Spirit-Led Ministry

In the 21st Century

Empowered Preaching, Teaching, Healing and Leading

Thomson K. Mathew

Copyright © 2004 by Thomson K. Mathew

Spirit-Led Ministry in the 21st Century
by Thomson K. Mathew

Printed in the United States of America

ISBN 1-594673-65-9

All rights reserved by the author. The contents and views expressed in this book are solely those of the author and are not necessarily those of Xulon Press, Inc. The author guarantees this book is original and does not infringe upon any laws or rights, and that this book is not libelous, plagiarized or in any other way illegal. If any portion of this book is fictitious, the author guarantees it does not represent any real event or person in a way that could be deemed libelous. No part of this book may be reproduced in any form without the permission of the author.

Scripture texts used in this book, unless otherwise indicated, are taken from *New International Version*; copyright © 1978 by the New York International Bible Society.

To

*Molly, Amy, and Jamie Mathew
For their love*

And

*Oral, Evelyn, Richard and Lindsay Roberts
For their trust*

FOREWORD

Currently there is a plethora of books, journals and magazines dealing with the subject of the role of a pastor including preaching, teaching, healing and leading. Most of these books are written by leading evangelical ministries. Their works are well done and insightful, but often underemphasize the Holy Spirit's work in these roles.

There is a great need for information on ministry from a Pentecostal/Charismatic dimension. This book by Dr. Thomson Mathew meets that need. Here is a well trained and experienced Pentecostal/Charismatic pastor, chaplain and theological educator, writing out of years of experience, about roles of the minister with a balanced emphasis. We now have a textbook quality guide to add to the current offering of books on the subject. This book will satisfy the academic and practical aspects of the ministry.

Undergirding Dr. Mathew's four major roles of a minister are two strong foundational stones— character and skills. In Psalm 78:72 we read, "And David shepherded them with <u>integrity of heart; with skillful hands he led them.</u>" These twins of balance are found in each of the roles delineated by Thomson Mathew. In fact, he practices this balance in his own life and teaches them by his example. Really, what good are skills if they are not accompanied by character of heart, and how effective is a person with character minus skills?

This book is both cutting edge and basic. May its truths impact today's pastors in an ever changing and sometimes dangerous world, one that desperately needs ministers with integrity (character) and skills.

Kenneth Mayton
Assistant Dean for Doctoral Studies
School of Theology and Missions
Oral Roberts University

INTRODUCTION

For a number of years now, I have felt the need for a book on Pentecostal/Charismatic ministry that is biblically sound and theologically balanced. I am not the only one who has struggled to find textbooks for ministerial students that seriously consider the work of the Holy Spirit in ministry. While there are plenty of books on ministry in general and various aspects of ministry in particular, there is a tremendous shortage of books on ministry from a Pentecostal/Charismatic perspective. Most books on ministry coming out of mainline denominations do not pay adequate attention to the role of the Holy Spirit in ministry. Many of the books on ministry written by Trinitarian Christians are in effect binitarian in viewpoint. And many of them seem to be afraid to deal with the Church's ministry of healing. In many books, there is a total neglect of the testimony of more than half a billion Christians in the world who bear witness to the current move of the Holy Spirit through conversions, signs, wonders, and miracles.

I have been teaching courses in ministry and pastoral care at Oral Roberts University School of Theology and Missions for more than fifteen years. My students have asked me to put into writing some of the material I have been teaching. Being a seminary administrator all these years, there never was a convenient time to do so. Finally, I came to the conclusion that there never would be a convenient time and I started to put these pages together.

This is not a comprehensive book on Spirit-led ministry. However, I have attempted to present a theology of ministry that is faithful to the Bible and the history of the Church and that takes into account the work of the Holy Spirit NOW. I have also attempted to cover the four major things Jesus asked His followers to do— teach, preach, heal, and lead. I have presented these topics from a pneumatological perspective and in light of the challenges posed by the postmodern twenty-first century.

I have not written an original treatise. These pages contain ideas I gleaned from many people. In addition to my own teachers, and authors I have read, I owe much to the theological faculty at Oral Roberts University. We have spent countless hours in the last few years discussing and debating what biblical ministry ought to look like today. We have argued about what a Spirit-led minister— the intended product of our seminary—should be like. Particularly, I want to mention the following colleagues who have inspired me and challenged me as I worked with them and co-taught with them: Howard M. Ervin, for his insights on healing as a sign of the Kingdom of God; Trevor Grizzle, for his study of preaching in the New Testament; Charles Snow, for his grasp of Pentecostal ministry and preaching; Kenneth Mayton, for his understanding of the challenges posed by the twenty-first century; and Edward Decker, for never allowing his colleagues to forget the context in which our graduates will be ministering.

I am indebted to several individuals who made this work possible. My wife Molly and daughters Amy and Jamie are at the top of this list. I read and wrote at their expense. They were patient and long-suffering. My administrative assistant, Judy Cope, volunteered numerous hours, typing and proofreading major parts of this book. Two students— Katharina Bastian and Shelly-Ann Peart— offered skillful editorial assistance. Ruth McIntosh and Susan George gave significant editorial assistance. I am extremely grateful to all these persons.

Probably my greatest qualification for writing this book is that I am a third-generation Pentecostal minister whose ancestors were St. Thomas Christians of India. My father and grandfather were Pentecostal preachers in South India. My wife's father and grandfather were also Pentecostal preachers there. My father-in-law pastored one church for forty years in Kayamkulam, Kerala State, India. My father pastored his last church for thirty years as he supervised thirty other churches in Mavelikara District of Kerala, India. I grew up in Indian Pentecostal parsonages until I came to America in 1972. After my studies at Yale Divinity School, I pastored a growing Pentecostal church in New Haven, Connecticut for five years. My brother and my wife's brother are pastors. All four of my sisters are married to pastors. All these relationships, experiences, and observations have influenced this writing.

My father and last living parent passed away in 2002. At the funeral service held at the church he pastored, I spoke, as the eldest child of six, about our family's self-understanding, making reference to the conversation between Joseph's brothers and the Pharaoh in Egypt: "Pharaoh asked the brothers, 'What is your occupation?' 'Your servants are shepherds,' they replied to Pharaoh, 'just as our fathers were'" (Gen. 47:3). This book is written from the perspective of a shepherd, one who is concerned about evangelistic as well as pastoral ministry. I hope it will be seen as a strength of this work.

The modern Pentecostal movement is a hundred years old now. The pioneers of the movement faced their day and gave their very best. I believe that the movement now requires better trained leaders, with passion and competence, who can address the challenges of their own day. I have accepted the preparation of such ministers as the calling and mission of my life. This book is a humble contribution toward that mission.

Chancellor Oral Roberts and President Richard Roberts of Oral Roberts University have repeatedly challenged their theological faculty to develop a reputable school for the training of Spirit-led ministers, where persons who are called by God can "get their learning and keep their burning." I hope ORU School of Theology and Missions is that kind of a school, and that this book describes such a ministry.

If a current pastor or future minister receives an insight or a sense of encouragement by reading these pages, I will be more than grateful. I submit these pages to God for His purposes.

Thomson K. Mathew
School of Theology and Missions
Oral Roberts University
Tulsa, Oklahoma, USA
Spring 2004

CONTENTS

Foreword vii
Introduction ix

CHAPTER 1
 MINISTRY DEFINED 17
  Biblical Metaphors 20
  Ministry of Jesus 21
  Jesus the Model 23
  Empowered Life 24
  Ministry as Leadership 26
  Ministry as Relationship 28
  Ministry as Tasks 29
  Call and Authority 29
  Ministry and the Kingdom of God 30
  Hope Bearing 33
  Minister as Messenger 34
  Ministry: Revealing the Heart of God 36
  Rewards of Ministry 36

CHAPTER 2
 A HISTORY OF CHRISTIAN MINISTRY 39
  Prototype: Ministry in Acts 44
  History of Shepherding 48
  A Thematic History 58
  Ministry in America 60
  Twentieth Century Pentecostal
  Ministry 61
  Ministry and Dominant Social
  Characters 64

CHAPTER 3
CHALLENGES OF THE NEW CENTURY 67
Contemporary Images of Ministry 67
Cultural Challenges 69
Exegeting the World 74
Difficulties in Ministry 79
Evangelism in the New Age 79
Seven Forces 80
Need for True Revival 84
Need for Integrity 87
Problem of Denial 89

CHAPTER 4
MINISTRY AND THE HOLY SPIRIT 93
Nouwen's View 95
Spirit-filled Ministry 96
Empowerment 99
Authority from Jesus 100
The Authority of the Word of God 103
Need-meeting Church 104
Disciple-making Church 108
A Spirit-filled Church 109
Authority and Accountability 111
Prosperity 112
A Healthy Congregation 114

CHAPTER 5
COMPETENT CHARISMATIC MINISTRY 121
Competency: A Methodist Model 122
Style of Ministry 124
Being Healthy in Ministry 125
Ministry to Families 128
Ministry to Women 132
Ministry to Children 135

　　　　　　Institutional Ministry 136
　　　　　　Praise and Worship Ministry 141
　　　　　　Continuing Education of Ministers..........145

CHAPTER 6
PREACHING IN THE POWER OF THE SPIRIT..153
　　　　　　Eight Preaching Principles.......................160
　　　　　　A Sample Pentecostal Sermon.................166

CHAPTER 7
TEACHING AS JESUS TAUGHT 175
　　　　　　Jesus, Teaching, and the Holy Spirit........176
　　　　　　Educational Philosophy 177
　　　　　　Good Teaching..179
　　　　　　Adult Education 180
　　　　　　Teaching Teens...184
　　　　　　Teaching for Daily Decisions 187
　　　　　　Types of Faith 189
　　　　　　Theological Reflection.............................190
　　　　　　Church as a Theological Seminary 193

CHAPTER 8
THE HEALING MINISTRY IN THE NEW CENTURY..197
　　　　　　Faith and Healing.....................................200
　　　　　　Signs and Wonders 203
　　　　　　Evangelistic Versus Pastoral Healing......205
　　　　　　Theological Presuppositions....................207
　　　　　　Healing in the Local Church....................210

CHAPTER 9
POWER-FILLED SERVANT LEADERSHIP 213
　　　　　　Next Stage of Leadership.........................214

    New Paradigm 215
    Biblical Language of Leadership 216
    Secrets of Success 216
    Management Versus Leadership 218
    Conflict Resolution 218
    Limits of Ministry 219
    Effective Leadership 220
    A Spirit-led Model 221

CHAPTER 10
A CALL TO EXCELLENCE 231

ENDNOTES 235

BIBLIOGRAPHY 243

CHAPTER 1

MINISTRY DEFINED

As the Church of Jesus Christ enters a new millennium, Christian ministry faces many challenges. Several studies have shown that ministry today is a hazardous profession. Contemporary society takes a toll on ministers and their families; major denominations are losing ministers, and recent studies indicate that the percentage of younger ministers in these denominations is very low. People who enter ministry with great enthusiasm and expectations seem to burn out as the result of multiple demands. How does one minister in such a context, and how can institutions prepare people for successful ministry? This book is an effort to address such questions.

Ministry can be viewed through biblical, historical, and theological perspectives. We will begin this discussion with a biblical definition of Christian ministry.

Since Christian ministry must be guided by its biblical mandates at all times, it is appropriate to begin with the scriptural texts. First, Christian ministry is a total response to God's call on a person's life (2 Tim. 1:9, 1 Thess. 2:12). While the Bible acknowledges the priesthood of all believers, it clearly indicates that God calls certain individuals for specific offices of ministry. In *The Purpose of the*

Church and Its Ministry, Richard Niebuhr outlines four distinct calls in the life of a minister.[1] The first is the call to become a Christian. The future minister receives an additional secret call, followed by a providential call that manifests itself through gifts and talents. Finally, the minister receives an ecclesiastical call that publicly acknowledges God's call upon his or her life. In this stage, God's call is affirmed by the body of Christ and is confirmed through ordination.

Scripture defines ministry as being a co-worker with God, carrying out His purposes in the world (John 4:34, 2 Cor. 6:1). The Almighty God chooses to depend on fragile human beings to complete His work of restoration, reconciliation, and redemption in this fallen world. Ministry is, therefore, doing God's will in the world. Before God's will can be carried out, it must be sought in prayer. Ministry, then, is doing God's will through one's life, while one is seeking that will in prayer (1 John 2:17).

Ordained ministers are not required to carry out all of the practical aspects of ministry. God gave apostles, prophets, evangelists, pastors, and teachers for the equipping of the saints to do the work of the ministry, according to Ephesians 4:12. To a large degree, ministry is simply equipping and enabling other believers to fulfill the multiple ministries of God's church. The ultimate purpose of ministry is, therefore, to produce people who minister. Although not all are called to the offices of ministry, all believers are called to serve. True ministry is enabling others to serve in the Name of Jesus, by edifying, building, equipping, and helping them to grow.

Ministry involves bringing men and women into a vital relationship with God through Jesus Christ (Corinthians 5:20). It is also the proclamation (*kerygma*) of the Gospel of Jesus Christ (2 Tim. 4:2, 5). As people are reconciled with God, they are also called to become reconciled with each other; therefore, one can say that biblical ministry is a relational enterprise.

Scripture confirms that ministry is bringing wholeness to individuals: "May your whole spirit, soul, and body be kept blameless at the coming of our Lord Jesus Christ" (1 Thess. 5:23). The well-being and wholeness of individuals is God's will. According to this reference, biblical wholeness is holiness. We are sanctified to be whole; therefore ministry must seek to restore persons to wholeness by bringing healing in body, mind, and spirit. True ministry can only be accomplished through a life of servanthood to God and others in the Name of Christ (Gal. 5:13, 6:2, 5). *Diakonia* means service. The highest title in the Kingdom of God is that of servant; thus leadership in God's church must be empowered servant leadership.

Scripture also emphasizes the importance of *koinonia,* the fellowship of believers and the communion of saints (1 John 1:7). Ministry involves facilitating this fellowship and communion in the body of Christ.

In essence, ministry is the call of God on one's life. According to Ephesians 4, a minister is a gift of God to the church, a representative of God who pleads with the world to be reconciled with God. A minister, as an ambassador, must dialogue with the world, while at the same time remaining in constant communication with God. The pastoral epistles further illustrate ministerial duties, including reproving, rebuking, exhorting, enduring, and doing the work of an evangelist. They also describe equipping, perfecting, edifying, unifying, and bringing persons to maturity.

BIBLICAL METAPHORS

The Gospels are filled with images of ministry and discipleship. David W. Bennett, in *Metaphors of Ministry,* categorizes these as images of people and images of things.[2] Some images are relationship-oriented, while others are task-oriented. Relationship-oriented images include those of brother, sister, child, son, friend, guest, and disciple. Images of servant, manager, shepherd, worker, apostle, witness, and fisherman illustrate task-oriented metaphors. Scripture uses commonplace things such as soil, field, firstfruits, vine and branches, wheat, sheep, salt, light, building, and body to bear the image of ministry.

From these images Bennett draws certain metaphoric themes. First, he sees the theme of weakness and dependence in biblical ministry. The minister is a weak vessel on his own, but can depend on God for strength. Bennett sees a second theme of honor and dignity in biblical ministry. It is an honor to be a minister of the Gospel, and God calls us to be vessels of honor. We bring glory to God when we serve honorably. Bennett also sees the theme of interconnection in biblical ministry, in images such as branch, building, and body. Ministry involves connecting people to God and connecting people to people. Ministers connect people in a disconnected world, which makes ministry inclusive work rather than exclusive.

A minister fulfills many roles. Functionally, he or she participates in the community and engages in doing the tasks needed within the community. Regardless of his position, a minister is a person who serves under authority; all authority is given to him, but he is not to become authoritarian. God alone initiates an individual's call to ministry, and he or she chooses whether to respond. All believers have equal worth in the Kingdom of God, but all have different areas of responsibility. Ultimately, we are called to identify with Jesus in the pattern of His life, and we are accountable to God for our character and service.

MINISTRY OF JESUS

During a lecture, Colin Cruse of the University of Melbourne identified the following characteristics of Jesus' ministry:
1. Clarity of purpose – Jesus had a clear understanding of the purpose of his life.
2. Authority – Jesus was aware of His total authority and His self limitation of that authority.
3. Servant style – Jesus adopted a servant-leader model of ministry.
4. Powerful spiritual dynamics – Jesus was empowered by the Holy Spirit to fulfill His purpose.

Jesus' ministry contains the following themes according to Cruse:
1. Apostleship – Jesus was one who was sent by God.
2. Servanthood – Jesus came to serve, not to be served.
3. The role of the Spirit – The Holy Spirit was active in Jesus' life and ministry.

Jesus was an apostle of God, who came to proclaim and inaugurate the Kingdom of God. An apostle is one who is sent. The Father sent Jesus, and Jesus sent twelve envoys. We are to receive Him and those whom He sent. "Let us go . . . That is why I have come" (Mark 1:38). We know that He was sent specifically to the Jews, because He said, "I was sent only to the lost sheep of Israel" (Matt. 15:24). Jesus was sent like a prophet, but He was greater than a prophet because of the one who sent Him. Scripture tells us that those who received the disciples also received Jesus: "He who receives you receives me" (Matt. 10:40).

Jesus was the ideal servant, fulfilling the biblical prophecies of the Suffering Servant. The disciples were to follow His example of servanthood (John 13:5), because Jesus instructed them not to "lord it over" others (Matt. 20:25-28). Among His disciples, the greatest one was to become the servant of all (Matt. 23:11).

Jesus' ministry was powerful because of the presence and power of the Holy Spirit in His life. Even before His birth, the Holy Spirit overshadowed Mary (Luke 1:35), and Jesus was conceived by the Spirit (Matt. 1:20, 23). The Holy Spirit came upon Jesus at the time of His baptism (Mark 1:8-11), and the Spirit drove Jesus to the wilderness (Luke 4:1). He returned from the wilderness in the power of the Holy Spirit (Luke 4:14), empowered by the Holy Spirit to carry out His ministry (Mark 13:11, Matt. 10:20, Luke 12:12, John 14:15-17, John 15:26). Jesus promised the outpouring of the Holy Spirit on His disciples (Luke 24:49); thus the ministry of the disciples was also characterized by the empowerment of the Holy Spirit. The Spirit was to enable them to speak (Mark 13:11), to testify, and to bear witness. Jesus, the apostle, the servant, and the one who is led by the Spirit, is the ministry role model for His disciples, and for all those who will follow their example.

David McKenna, in *Renewing Our Ministry,* describes the relationship between the minister and Jesus Christ, stating that Jesus Christ calls His ministers to be trustworthy, teachable, and task-oriented.[3]

According to McKenna, Christ is our model of trustworthiness as He shows us the persons we can be. He is our mentor as He teaches us truth. Christ is also our enabler who helps us to be effective in what we do. As followers, we imitate Christ, and as partakers of the divine nature, we personify Him.

Christ is our mentor who calls us to be teachable teachers, says McKenna, and He is also the One who calls us to be task-oriented. Ministry involves both leading and managing. Leadership focuses on effectiveness, so a good leader ensures that the correct tasks are carried out. A manager's focus is on efficiency, ensuring that the tasks are accomplished in a productive manner. A leader articulates the vision, and the manager implements it.

JESUS THE MODEL

Jesus is our model in the area of pastoral ministry. In *Jesus the Pastor,* John W. Frye identifies the characteristics of Jesus as a model shepherd.[4] Jesus had a strong sense of identity; He knew who He was and what He was called to do. This sense of identity enabled Him to focus on His destiny and purpose. Significantly, Jesus did not depend on His ministerial performance to settle His identity; His father affirmed Him before He performed the first miracle, saying "You are my Son, whom I love; with you I am well pleased" (Luke 3:22). Jesus' identity was not performance-based; rather it was rooted in Father God. Many ministers fall into the trap of performance-based identity, but a biblical model of ministry is anchored in God and in His call on the minister's life.

Jesus was empowered by the Spirit because the Spirit of the Lord was upon Him to preach the good news. Jesus was the incarnational presence of God to the degree that those around him could say, "We beheld His glory." As a shepherd He had a compassionate heart; thus He went about His Father's work, ministering to the oppressed. He was spiritually disciplined and committed to a community, but Jesus was also committed to telling the truth at all costs. He was not afraid of the devil, but he did take the power of evil seriously. He also shared authority with His disciples, because He found fulfillment in empowering others. He knew that sharing His authority did not diminish it.

EMPOWERED LIFE

The Bible clearly illustrates that an encounter with God is a prerequisite for ministry and empowerment. Abraham, the father of all who believe, had an encounter with the living God (Gen. 17:1-6). Similarly, Moses experienced a powerful encounter with God on the far side of the desert at Horeb (Exod. 3:1-7). Moses trained Joshua, but prior to the commencement of Joshua's leadership he also had an encounter with God.

> After the death of Moses the servant of the Lord, the Lord said to Joshua son of Nun, Moses' aide: "Moses my servant is dead. Now then, you and all these people, get ready to cross the Jordan River into the land I am about to give to them— to the Israelites . . . . As I was with Moses, so I will be with you; I will never leave you nor forsake you" (Josh. 1:1, 2, 5).

Samuel, the great Old Testament prophet, had an encounter with God while he was still a child (1 Sam. 3:4). He heard God's voice when the sons of Eli the priest did not. We read that the word of the Lord came down to Elijah (1 Kings 17:2) and launched him into a great ministry of service to God and His people. Elisha also heard from the Lord (2 Kings 7:1). During a dramatic encounter, Isaiah encountered God in the year Uzziah died (Isa. 6:1). He had a glimpse of God's holiness, which confronted his own inadequacies, causing him to cry out, "Woe to me." Isaiah experienced the touch of God's fire and responded to His call, "Whom shall I send? And who will go for us?" Individual encounters with God continued to occur in the New Testament. Saul of Tarsus encountered the living Savior and experienced a transformed life; the persecutor became the preacher of the Gospel.

A sense of call is a definite requirement of empowered ministry. An individual does not call himself; he or she is called by God. His only responsibility is to respond. Jonah tried to run away from God's call, but God won the race. God is still calling today. The harvest is ripe but the laborers are few; those who have heard God's call must respond.

Various theologians have tried to define ministry. Henri Nouwen stated that ministry involves teaching, preaching, counseling, organizing, and celebration.[5] Victor Furnish says that ministry is monitoring, maintaining, and strengthening the community of faith, as well as *koinonia* (fellowship), *eucharista* (celebration), and *diakonia* (service).[6] Mark, the evangelist, outlines Jesus' example of ministry: "He appointed twelve— designating them apostles— that they might be with him and that he might send them out to preach and to have authority to drive out demons" (Mark 3:14-15). Jesus illustrates that performance is of secondary importance to the primary call of the disciple *to be with Him*. We are called to preach and to drive out demons, but being with Jesus is our first priority. We are set apart to be with Him and to set the captives free.

Most contemporary theological writings lack the supernatural aspect of Christian ministry, but New Testament ministry embodies Spirit-led preaching, teaching, healing, and leading. We are called to do something beyond our own abilities, and we are empowered to do it through God's Holy Spirit. We cannot afford to be like all other helping professions. We deal not only with the natural aspect of life; we also must deal with the supernatural aspect that includes signs, wonders, healing, and miracles. We represent God and do His work as the Holy Spirit enables us.

MINISTRY AS LEADERSHIP

A minister is a leader of God's people, yet leadership has often been overlooked in the past as a vital aspect of ministry. In this regard, Moses is once again a fine example of a minister in leadership. Moses clearly led God's people, God Himself having chosen him for leadership. Eight distinctive leadership characteristics are evident in Moses' life and ministry:

1. **Hearing God:** Moses was a man who had a listening ear for God's voice. From the time he heard the voice coming out of the burning bush, Moses continually desired to hear God. Even when God's message was stern, Moses listened to it carefully.

2. **Obeying God:** Listening to God is very different from obeying Him. Moses was not only a listener but also an obedient servant of God. Moses followed God's directives very closely, with the exception of one occasion. As a leader, he represented God and implemented His wishes among the people. Although people were often offended, Moses gave priority to God's opinion of him.

3. **Confronting Evil:** Moses was not afraid to confront evil. He was willing to look the oppressor in the face and command him to let God's people go. Human power did not intimidate this man of God.

He knew that the Egyptian leader could destroy his body, but not his spirit.

4. **Correcting the Saints:** Moses was willing to correct the saints when they needed correction. He rebuked and disciplined them as needed, because he knew that he served a holy God whom he wanted his people to please.

5. **Interceding for the People:** Moses implemented rough discipline because in his heart he was a caring shepherd. He had to be both prophet and priest at the same time. As prophet he told the people, "Thus saith the Lord"; as priest he cried out before God on behalf of his people by standing in the gap for them.

6. **Being Human:** Many leaders try to act as if they are very different from their people. Some act as though they are spiritually superior and have a secret chat line to God that others do not have. Unfortunately much of this spiritual superiority is not authentic. Moses was a man of God, but he remained human before his people. The glory of God was on his face, yet he lived his daily life among the people as a human being. He experienced emotions of happiness, sadness, and anger, like any other human being, but he knew he was their leader, and the people knew it, too.

7. **Mentoring Others:** Many leaders are self-absorbed and shortsighted, assuming that they will be present to lead forever. Moses was different. He mentored others in leadership by training them to assume

leadership in the future. He wanted to ensure that there would not be a leadership vacuum after his death. Many present-day organizations experience a leadership vacuum when people have not been mentored in leadership.

8. **Developing Anointed Leaders:** Moses shared responsibility and authority with others. He allowed them to assist him in his work and in that process trained them for future responsibilities. When the time came, Joshua was ready to follow him in leadership. Joshua was not overwhelmed by the task because he was properly trained through mentoring and shepherding.

I believe that Moses' leadership qualities are important for all Christian leaders, whether they are professors or pastors. Although many individuals hold offices in ministry today, there is a shortage of good leaders among us. A political process will not create this type of leader; only a biblical model of leadership training will produce leaders who follow in the footsteps of Moses.

MINISTRY AS RELATIONSHIP

Ministry is a relational enterprise. One could say that God so loved the world that He established a relationship with the world through His son Jesus. Christians are called to stay in relationship with God and to invite others into such a relationship, as part of God's work of reconciliation. Our job is to plead with the world, "Be reconciled to God."

God made man in His own image. In the beginning, harmonious relationships existed not only between Adam and God and between Adam and Eve, but Adam also had peace with himself. Sin broke down all of these relationships. Adam became afraid of God and ashamed of himself, and he began to blame Eve for his problems. Fear, shame, and blame became part of the dynamics of life for the first humans, and have carried over into dysfunctional families today. Jesus Christ came into the world to reconcile these and other relationships that have been broken due to sin. Ministry is the vehicle through which this work is done; it is relational work.

MINISTRY AS TASKS

Ministry, as with all leadership, also involves tasks as well as relationships. The tasks of ministry relate to the mission and ministries of the church. The primary mission of the church is to evangelize (Matt. 28:18-20) and make disciples (2 Tim. 2:2). The ministries of the church include worship (John 4:24), The Word (2 Tim. 3:16), prayer (Eph. 6:18), and fellowship (Heb. 10:23-25). The ordinances (1 Cor. 11:23, 24; Mark 16:16) of the church are part of worship, while preaching, teaching, and counseling have to do with the ministry of the Word. All of these ministries require careful management, which involves planning, organizing, leading, and quality control.

CALL AND AUTHORITY

Any attempt to define ministry must address the concept of ministerial authority. What is the source of a minister's authority? What model of authority should he or she adopt? Individuals often imitate models of authority found in the business world and the military, yet the minister is to follow Jesus' model of authority. Jesus did not disclaim His authority, but made it clear that it belonged to Him (Luke 4:32). His authority came from God and therefore did not conform to the lower authority of this world (John 8:28).

"Jesus called them together and said, 'You know that the rulers of the Gentiles lord it over them, and their high officials exercise authority over them. Not so with you. Instead, whoever wants to become great among you must be your servant, and whoever wants to be first must be your slave–just as the Son of Man did not come to be served, but to serve, and to give his life as a ransom for many'" (Matt. 20:25-28).

His authority made Jesus a servant. All authority was given to Him, but Jesus Himself imposed limitations on how He exercised that authority (Matt. 4:1-11; 20:20-28). Similarly, Jesus willingly shared His authority with His disciples.

A minister's authority, according to Niebuhr, comes from God's call.[7] According to Samuel Southard, the sources of authority for a minister are obedience to God's call, the lordship of Jesus, the Church—the body of Christ, and legal authority.[8] Southard also states that ministerial authority manifests itself in five different ways: prophetic, evangelistic, pastoral, priestly, and organizational.[9] Godly character confirms a minister's authority, since character is formed in a person as he submits to authority. The centurion in the Gospel understood this mystery. He had authority because he was under authority. Similarly, a minister of the Gospel has authority because he or she is under authority. Paul exhorts ministers, "Follow me as I follow Christ."

MINISTRY AND THE KINGDOM OF GOD

Christian ministry must be seen in light of Jesus' teaching on the Kingdom of God. John the Baptist came announcing the arrival of the Kingdom, and Jesus proclaimed that it had arrived, saying, "Repent, for the kingdom of heaven is at hand" (Matt.3:2; 4:17 NKJV). John was beheaded and Jesus was crucified, but the disciples took up the same message of the Kingdom (Luke 9:1-6). The New Testament illustrates that the preaching of the Kingdom continued through the apostles, as seen in Paul's ministry (Rom. 14:17).

The Kingdom has three dimensions of time. In one respect, the Kingdom of God has already come and is currently at hand (Matt. 4:17; Luke 10:8, 9). Scripture states that the Kingdom of God is a present reality in our midst (Luke 17:21). The Kingdom of God also has a cosmic future dimension that has not yet fully come. The Kingdom of God is a mystery, but the parables of Jesus give us clues which lead us to gain understanding. For example, the Kingdom has a different value system; in the Kingdom, giving is the way to receive (Luke 6:38). The last shall be first in the Kingdom (Mark 10:31).

> If anyone would come after me, he must deny himself and take up his cross and follow me. For whoever wants to save his life will lose it, but whoever loses his life for me and for the gospel will save it (Mark 8:34, 35).

In the Kingdom, dying is the way to live, and losing is the way to gain.

Jesus uses the examples of a mustard seed and yeast to represent the Kingdom of God as a living organism that grows. As the mustard seed grows into a tree in which the birds of the air come to perch, and as the yeast spreads throughout a batch of dough, so the Kingdom of God must increase (Matt. 13:31-33). God allows good and bad to coexist in His Kingdom, just as good seeds grow with the tares (Matt. 13:24-26). The Master allows the weeds to remain for a season, "Because while you are pulling the weeds, you may root up the wheat with them" (Matt. 13:29). But a day will come when the weeds will be tied up in bundles to be burned and "The angels will come and separate the wicked from the righteous and throw them into the fiery furnace, where there will be weeping and gnashing of teeth" (Matt. 13:49-50). The Kingdom is also like a fisherman's net pulled up on the shore, full of good fish along with bad ones. The Kingdom of Heaven will also be like ten virgins who took their lamps and went out to meet the bridegroom; five of them were foolishly unprepared for His coming, but five of them had wisely prepared.

The Kingdom of God is a powerful entity. God reigns in His Kingdom, and the Kingdom's power is derived from the King. The resources of the Kingdom may not always manifest in silver and gold, but the Name of Jesus always holds power. Christian ministry is kingdom work, and as a citizen of the Kingdom a minister has access to the power and resources of the Kingdom of God. The book of Acts demonstrates the manifestation of the power of the Kingdom of God over and over again. This book chronicles the power of God, the power of His Spirit, the power of holiness, and the power of holy giving. We are admonished to seek God's Kingdom first; all other things shall be added unto us (Matt. 6:33). The Kingdom of God may not always appear attractive from the outside; in fact, it may be deceptively unattractive. A man who finds a piece of land with a treasure hidden in it goes and sells all he has in order to buy that field. A merchant looking for fine pearls finds one of great worth and sells all of his possessions in order to acquire it (Matt. 13:44-46). The behavior of these men makes no sense to the outside observer, who wonders what they could possibly have found that would cause them to give all that they have. Yet for the men who made the transaction the answer is clear: They have found treasure beyond description.

HOPE BEARING

Spirit-filled ministry is multifaceted. A Spirit-filled minister is a born-again person, who is filled with the Holy Spirit and called by God for His purposes. This is an individual who is in dialogue with God and man at the same time; his ministry embodies his identity as a believer. A Spirit-filled minister must have congruence and integrity in his life, in order to maintain a healthy balance of love and power. A person is congruent when he practices what he preaches. He has integrity when his word can be trusted. A loving person is not necessarily an empowered person, and a person who moves in the power of the Holy Spirit may, unfortunately, be lacking in love. Love increases as one connects with God Who is the source of love. Reading God's Word and meditating on the character of God helps one connect with God. Reflecting on God's love as it was displayed on the cross of Jesus deepens our understanding of God's love.

A Spirit-led minister must seek to be both a reflective practitioner and a grassroots theologian, who allows his actions to be guided by the Holy Spirit and by his personal reflection on the Word of God. The Word, the Spirit, and the community of faith provide the authority and the balance he needs. He is attuned to the Spirit of God through an on-going dialogue with God, with the help of the Spirit. In order to instill hope in others, he must have experienced God's saving and healing power in some form. The Spirit-filled minister must also be willing to test all things by the Word of God and reject those things not affirmed by God's Word. It is crucial that this individual care deeply for others. The Word of God must be the final authority in his life.

A minister will be identified by the message of hope that he conveys. I recall growing up in a parsonage in Kerala, India, where merchants sold all types of produce from door to door. Salesmen came to the door and announced their wares, then moved on to the next house. My grandmother sometimes missed the salesman and had to call after him. She would call him by whatever he was carrying on his head to sell, such as "Mr. Banana" or "Mr. Coconut." Of course, these were not the names of the merchants, but they always responded. They were identified by what they were carrying. A minister is a bearer of hope; we carry Christ in us, the hope of glory.

MINISTER AS MESSENGER

Old Testament prophets and New Testament apostles are often viewed as role models for ministry. Ministers, as carriers of God's message, can also follow the model of Gabriel, the angel. Gabriel spoke to Zechariah the prophet, saying,

> I am Gabriel. I stand in the presence of God, and I have been sent to speak to you and to tell you this good news. And now you will be silent and not able to speak until the day this happens, because you did not believe my words, which will come true at their proper time (Luke 1:19, 20).

Gabriel, as a messenger for God, described his ministry to Zechariah as: (1) standing in the presence of God, (2) being sent to speak good news, and (3) waiting in expectation for the fulfillment of God's Word.

Ministry involves all three aspects of Gabriel's work, yet the hardest part of ministry is standing in the presence of God and waiting for His timing. The Bible uses two different Greek words for the concept of time. The word *chronos* denotes chronological or ordinary time, whereas the word *kairos* represents God's time or the fullness of time. Ministry demands that we patiently wait for God's timing.

The presentation of God's message is not risk free. Those who share God's Word risk not only the rejection of that Word by the hearers, but also the possibility of that message not being fulfilled within one's own time frame. For example, the prophet Isaiah gave a word from the Lord to King Hezekiah concerning the king's impending death. The prophet clearly heard from God and was faithful to present what he heard. Hezekiah, however, repented and God extended his life. It appeared that the prophet's initial word did not come to pass.

Since God is not confined to man's time or space, ministry often involves times and seasons that require patience. For example, Jonah did not want to go to Nineveh, but through unusual circumstances he eventually delivered the message God gave him. In spite of his initial reluctance to follow God's call, Jonah was faithful at last to deliver the word he received. When the people responded to Jonah's message, "God . . . had compassion and did not bring upon them the destruction he had threatened" (Jon. 3:10). Jonah was frustrated by this, but he learned that the nature of ministry involves being faithful to God and His Word, without taking offense at the consequences.

Time spent in God's presence and hearing His Word results in satisfaction, rather than frustration. Most often ministers are bearers of good news that does come to pass. They have the privilege to say that the blind will see, the deaf will hear, and the lame will walk. They can also encourage the weak to say, "I am strong," and the poor to say, "I am rich." Ministers can exhort the hurting, because they know the Lord's desire to bring healing to all people.

The minister of the Gospel is a herald who receives direction when he is in the presence of God. For instance, Moses' was commissioned as he stood in the presence of God on Mount Horeb. Samuel heard God's plans in His Temple. Ministers should strive to follow the model of Gabriel the messenger, being faithful to stand, speak, and expect.

MINISTRY: REVEALING THE HEART OF GOD

In summary, ministry is more than preaching, teaching, counseling, soul winning, or healing. It is also more than performing signs and wonders. Ministry involves an individual embodying the incarnational presence of Christ in a fragmented world, in obedience to God's call and in accordance with His will. In many ways ministry is simply revealing the heart of God. In order to minister effectively, one must dialogue with God and man at the same time. Ultimately, ministry is faithfulness to God, who has called us out of darkness into His marvelous light.

REWARDS OF MINISTRY

Scripture compares ministry to work in a vineyard because it is hard labor. Ministry is not for those who seek ease and comfort, but for individuals who are committed to working toward greater rewards. The parable of the laborers in the vineyard illustrates the truth that God will reward all His faithful servants (Matt. 20:1-15). Some came to work early in the morning; others came at the third hour, the sixth hour, and the eleventh hour. The Master told them he would pay them whatever was right. When the evening came, each one received the same pay regardless of his starting time, and those who came earlier began to complain. The Master responded:

Friend, I am not being unfair to you. Didn't you agree to work for a denarius? Take your pay and go. I want to give the man who was hired last the same as I gave you. Don't I have the right to do what I want with my own money? Or are you envious because I am generous? (Matt. 20:13-15).

Different interpretations of this passage exist, but one thing is very clear: A fair reward is promised to the faithful laborer. In fact, all laborers are rewarded equally. Scholars have struggled to understand this passage, because from a worldly perspective the pay scale seems unfair. I agree with William Willimon that a more reflective reading of the parable provides the deeper interpretation that the pay is Jesus Himself. Jesus is the ultimate reward, and no greater currency could be given to any worker. In other words, those who have Jesus have everything they need. "He who did not spare his own Son, but gave him up for us all–how will he not also, along with him, graciously give us all things?" (Rom. 8:32).

CHAPTER 2

A HISTORY OF CHRISTIAN MINISTRY

No one expected the small band of followers of a crucified Galilean to become the largest religious group in the world. It was natural for people to expect this sect to disband, as had similar groups led by Theudas, Judas, and the like (Acts 5:35-37), but God had other plans. The crucified Galilean was raised from the dead and his followers took the message of his resurrection all over the world. Kings and kingdoms responded to that message, and ultimately nations and continents were transformed by it. Some understood the message of Jesus, while others misunderstood its implications. Some used it for their own advantage; others abused it. The history of the world is intricately connected with the story of Jesus, and the history of ministry is the story of its messengers.

The New Testament contains only a few decades of Christian history. The primary group of Christians in Jerusalem, the church led by James, the brother of Jesus, was scattered as a result of persecution. These Jewish Christians spread the good news of Christ all over the world, but it was the impact of the Gentile-friendly church in Antioch that spread the message among the Gentiles. Eventually, Rome became the center of Christian activities. As the number of Christians increased, so did the degree of persecution. The second and third centuries were periods of severe Christian persecution.

The next period was an era in which the Christian church battled the pervasive influence of heresies against the Gospel message. Amazingly, many of those heresies are still in existence today, attempting to enter the mainstream of Christianity under different names and leaders. Many who refuse to study the history of the church keep repeating that history because they have not learned from past mistakes.

The Emperor Constantine's conversion and policies made Christianity a national religion. Yet, Christianity was not ready for such an upward mobility. Suddenly, half the population of the Roman Empire was Christian; their new status transformed Christianity from the religion of the persecuted to the religion of princes. The church as the Kingdom of God matched all other kingdoms in all possible ways! There was no longer a need to preach about the coming Kingdom of God when such a powerful kingdom, with so many benefits, was already at hand. The church went through a serious period of backsliding. During this era, organizational authority became more important to the church leadership than spiritual power.

As Church history continued, the world witnessed the formation of doctrines, heresies, monasticism, scholasticism, an East-West split, and unbiblical crusades. These were followed by the emergence of the Reformation, missionary movements, Holiness revivals, awakenings, revivalists, separatists, the Pentecostal movement, Ecumenism, and Spirit-led movements. All of these movements involved powerful personalities. Many settings became part of our Christian history: Jerusalem, Antioch, Rome, Constantinople,

Worms, Wales, Topeka, and Azusa, just to name a few. The various movements and their respective locations significantly impacted both the understanding and the practice of Christian ministry.

It is difficult to summarize the history of ministry, because any attempt to do so is inherently simplistic. One can state with confidence, however, that ministry in the apostolic age was Spirit-empowered. It emphasized preaching, teaching, and healing, with the presence of signs, wonders, and miracles. Signs and wonders confirmed the preaching of the Word. Persecution of the ministers was almost guaranteed during this period. This was the pattern of ministry from Jerusalem to Patmos, spanning Acts to Revelation.

During the period of the church fathers, ministry was characterized by a form of godliness rather than by spiritual power. Although the church provided sound and helpful teaching, ministry in those days was sacramental and symbolic. The emphasis was no longer on preaching, teaching, and healing, with accompanying signs, wonders, and miracles. Instead, the church established itself in codified doctrines and in the creation of hierarchies. Ministry also became more reclusive during this period, characterized by monks and monasteries. The nature of ministry was contemplative, and thus it was predominately detached from common people. Christian disciplines were developed during this time period, while clerical learning was also emphasized.

The longer period, often called the Dark Ages, preceded the Protestant Reformation. *Sola scriptura,* "only scripture," was the slogan of the reformers, and preaching became the primary focus of ministry. Ministers during the time of the Reformation were preachers who recaptured the preaching aspect of ministry from the New Testament. The preaching of salvation through faith in Jesus Christ became the primary task of ministry. The revivals that followed this message greatly impacted ministry. For example, Methodism emphasized discipleship and lay ministries. The awakenings produced preachers who emphasized conversion and holiness. Ministers were primarily concerned with saving souls. Although there were many full-time pastors, evangelists, and revivalists, lay persons also found ministry opportunities.

The evangelical and Holiness revivals of the eighteenth and nineteenth centuries set the stage for the Pentecostal movement in the early twentieth century. Beginning like a river with multiple streams, and eventually reaching throughout the world, the Pentecostal movement produced ministers who believed in the present-day operation of the Holy Spirit. They began to preach, teach, baptize, and lead people to the baptism in the Holy Spirit. They also rediscovered the gifts of the Holy Spirit and began to exercise those gifts in their ministries. The gift of speaking in tongues and the dramatic ministry of divine healing seemed to receive more attention than other operations of the Holy Spirit. Ministers were trained through mentoring and Bible institutes. They studied the Bible and learned practical ministries under the tutelage of experienced ministers. The beginning of the modern Pentecostal movement also witnessed ministry models that transcended color and gender. This period soon passed, as racially segregated, male-dominated denominations were formed. Pentecostals also began to go out into the world as Full Gospel missionaries, following the example of major missionary enterprises of the previous centuries. Missionary pastors took the Pentecostal message far and near, doing the work of shepherding as well as evangelizing and educating.

A new movement, called the Charismatic movement, began to emerge by the middle of the twentieth century. This complex movement impacted Catholics and Protestants alike.

Oral Roberts, founder and chancellor of Oral Roberts University, and Demos Shakarian, pioneer of the Full Gospel Businessmen's Fellowship International, were two of the leaders of this emerging movement. The Charismatic movement produced lay ministers who, as part of their Christian walk, evangelized and led people to receive the baptism of the Holy Spirit. Ministry was not limited to ordained clergy or identified churches; for all practical purposes the Charismatics underscored the concept of the priesthood of all believers. While the Pentecostals emphasized divine healing and the baptism in the Holy Spirit, with speaking in tongues as the initial physical evidence of Spirit baptism, the Charismatics gave priority to tongues as a prayer language, along with signs and wonders. Eventually, independent Charismatic churches, and Word, faith, and prosperity ministries came out of the Charismatic movement. Often leaders of these ministries were not Bible college graduates, but believers who had experienced what they were teaching and had been mentored by independent ministers. Many of the churches within the Charismatic movement became megachurches, led by pastors who saw themselves as "ranchers" rather than shepherds. These churches utilize cell groups or other small group models to meet the spiritual needs of the majority of their members. Churches generally train leaders for these small groups in basic ministry skills; many develop their own Bible institutes and ministry training centers to equip the large number of lay ministers they need.

The end of the twentieth century witnessed new openness for formal training and continuing education in ministry on the part of the Pentecostals and Charismatics. Today, many working pastors attend Bible colleges and seminaries to retool themselves for ministry in these challenging times. Pentecostal and Charismatic institutions of learning are responding to the increasing educational needs of this growing movement.

A brief review of the history of ministry during the last two millennia leads one to make the following observations. One can make two mistakes in ministry and ministry preparation. The first mistake is to neglect the life and power of the Holy Spirit in ministry; this produces lifeless traditions and a stale Church. On the other hand, it is also a major mistake to ignore the history of the church. Even those who are empowered by the Holy Spirit must learn the history of the Christian church, because ignorance of the past leads many to repeat the mistakes of the past. In other words, old heresies often show up as new teachings. People who have not studied their history take the risk of embracing such heresies as fresh revelations.

PROTOTYPE: MINISTRY IN ACTS

Ministry in the New Testament period clearly emphasized preaching, teaching, and healing, as well as signs, wonders, and miracles. A closer examination of the book of Acts provides a more detailed understanding of Spirit-empowered ministry. The book of Acts begins at the Ascension of Jesus. Jesus instructed the disciples to wait in Jerusalem until they received the power of the Holy Spirit, which would enable them to be witnesses from Jerusalem. The Holy Spirit came upon them on the day of Pentecost as Peter and the other apostles were ministering. The remainder of the book of Acts documents their Spirit-filled ministry.

One can discern five major themes that represent the thrust of Spirit-filled ministry in Acts: prayer as ministry, power-filled evangelism, response to persecution, praise and worship, and enhancing fellowship. The following overview of the book of Acts will examine these themes.

1. Ministry of Prayer

Prayer is a major theme of the book of Acts. The disciples pray in one place (Acts. 1:14) and in one accord (Acts 2:1). Prayer is offered at the ordination of deacons (Acts 6:6), and Peter and John pray for the Samaritans to receive the baptism of the Holy Spirit (Acts 8:14, 15). Saul prays and learns that Ananias is on his way to minister to him (Acts 9:11, 12), while Peter prays on a roof top and has a vision about God's plans for the Gentiles (Acts 10:9). The church prays for Peter during his imprisonment, and God answers their prayer (Acts 12:12). Similarly, Paul and Silas pray together in prison, and the prison doors open for them (Acts 16:25). The elders fast and pray on behalf of Paul and Barnabas in preparation for their ordination (Acts 13:2, 3), and Paul, on his way to prayer, meets Lydia who receives the Gospel (Acts 16:13, 14).

2. Power-Filled Evangelism

Power-filled evangelism is another theme of the book of Acts. Essentially, Acts represents an empowered community engaged in power-filled ministry. The power of the Holy Spirit comes (Acts 2:4), and shortly thereafter a lame man enters the temple walking and leaping after he is healed (Acts 3:6-8). Ananias and Sapphira lie to the Holy Spirit and encounter death (Acts 5:3-5). Prison doors open by the power of God (Acts 5:17-19), and other signs and wonders manifest in Samaria following the preaching of the gospel (Acts 8:5-8). Philip, the evangelist, is transported by the power of the Spirit (Acts 8:39); Peter walks out of the prison to join the assembled believers (Acts 12:7-11); and prison doors open for Paul and Silas (Acts 16:26). The woman with an evil spirit is delivered by the power of God (Acts 16:18), while the Gentile, Cornelius, and his household receive the power of the Holy Spirit (Acts 10:44-46).

The power experienced by the community of believers in the book of Acts is multifaceted. They have the power of the apostles' teaching and the power of the Holy Spirit; yet they also enjoy the power that comes from holy living and from a lifestyle of giving and receiving. Thus, the community is not only a powerful community, but also a love-filled community. Power and love are balanced in Acts so that ministry is more than the demonstration of power; it also includes the impartation of divine love.

3. Response to Persecution

Ministry in the book of Acts evokes persecution, and the disciples' response to that persecution becomes a part of their ministry. Peter is threatened (Acts 4:18-21), imprisoned (Acts 5:17, 18), and beaten (Acts 5:40, 41). Stephen is stoned, but before the first stone hits his body he looks up to heaven and sees the face of Jesus (Acts 7:55-60). Peter is imprisoned again after James is killed (Acts 12:1-3), while unbelievers plot to abuse Paul and Barnabas (Acts 14:5). Later, Paul and Silas are beaten and imprisoned (Acts 16:22, 23).

Scripture describes the apostles' response to their persecution, which has become an encouragement for persecuted believers throughout history. Peter rejoices for the privilege of suffering for the sake of the Gospel (Acts 5:41), and Stephen's martyrdom impacts Saul of Tarsus (Acts 7:58; 8:1). After the church prays in response to Peter's imprisonment and an angel releases Peter, he becomes a living witness of the power of God. In the midst of their circumstances, Paul and Silas minister to the bewildered jailer and to the confused prisoners who are caught in the miracle of the open prison (Acts 16:25-34). In the book of Acts persecution is an outcome of ministry, as well as a vehicle for ministry.

4. Praise and Worship

Ministry in the book of Acts consistently includes praise and worship of God. The disciples gather to praise and worship God in the upper room (Acts 2:1-4, 11), and the persecuted apostles praise God for the privilege of suffering (Acts 5:41). The healed lame man responds by walking, leaping, and praising God (Acts 3:8). The Ethiopian eunuch rejoices in his salvation (Acts 8:39), and the household of Cornelius praises God as the Spirit gives them utterance (Acts 10:44-46). During the imprisonment, the praises of God fill the prison so that it cannot contain God's servants (Acts 16:25, 26).

5. Fellowship

Christian fellowship (*koinonia*) is a key component in the book of Acts, and facilitating fellowship has always been a ministerial responsibility. Scripture describes the disciples as being together in one accord, in one place.

> They devoted themselves to the apostles' teaching and to the fellowship, to the breaking of bread and to prayer ... All the believers were together and had everything in common. Selling their possessions and goods, they gave to anyone as he had need. Every day they continued to meet together in the temple courts. They broke bread in their homes and ate together with glad and sincere hearts, praising God and enjoying the favor of all the people. And the Lord added to their number daily those who were being saved (Acts 2:42, 44-47).

It is clear that the earliest Christians believed in fellowship. They shared their life with each other, worshiped together, and suffered together. In the midst of persecution and challenges, they practiced Christian fellowship.

HISTORY OF SHEPHERDING

The history of Christian ministry is the continuing story of the ministry of Jesus of Nazareth. The Old Testament describes the shepherding ministry of prophets and priests who were servants of the Shepherd-God. The New Testament presents Jesus Christ as the Great Shepherd of the new covenant, who gave up His life for the sheep. He appointed apostles, prophets, evangelists, pastors, and teachers to continue His work of perfecting the saints. Pastor-teachers are to lead (Acts 20:28-31), guide (1 Pet. 2:25), instruct (1 Tim. 2:7), and correct (2 Tim. 4:2) the people of God. They are also instructed to feed (John 21:15), edify (2 Cor. 13:10), build up (Eph. 4:12), comfort (2 Cor. 1:3-4), rebuke (Tit. 1:13), warn (Acts 20:31), and watch over souls (Heb. 13:17).

Charles Ver Straten, in A *Caring Church*, sees the connection between the Old and New Testaments in the area of shepherding. He points out that Jesus, the Good Shepherd, *intentionally* trained His apostles to do the work of the ministry. Jesus ordained His disciples so that they could preach, teach, heal, and drive out demons (Matt. 9:36-38; Mk. 3:14, 15; 6:13), but New Testament ministry consisted of much more than action and performance; pastoral ministry in the New Testament was a ministry of the heart. According to Ver Straten, this ministry of the heart is demonstrated in the contrast between the Jewish elders, who were basically administrators, and the Christian elders, *presbyteros*, who were primarily shepherds.[1]

Church Fathers

The second century Church apparently viewed the bishop as the successor to the apostle. While this was a deviation from the practice of the primitive Church, it emphasizes the importance the early Church gave to pastoral work and ministry. The pastoral concern of the early Church is seen in Polycarp's description of the quailfications of a presbyter: "[They] must be compasssionate, merciful towards all men, turning back the sheep that are gone astray, visiting all the infirm, not neglecting a widow or an orphan or a poor man."[2]

The writings of the Church fathers provide clear evidence of the strong position of pastoral care in the ministry of the developing Church. Both the person of the minister and the ministerial method received their attention. Thomas Oden did a great service by providing a collection of these writings in his series entitled *Classical Pastoral Care*.[3] Gregory the Great, for instance, advised pastors to be people who "out of affection of heart sympathize with another's infirmity." John Chrysostom emphasized the importance of training for pastoral ministry:

> Anyone who is about to enter upon this ministry needs to explore it all thoroughly beforehand and only then to undertake this ministry. And why? Because if he studies the difficulties beforehand he will at any rate have the advantage of not being taken by surprise when they crop up.[4]

The shepherding metaphor is very evident in the writings of early fathers. Origen writes, "The good Shepherd makes it His business to seek for the best pastures for His sheep, and to find green and shady groves where they may rest during the noonday heat."[5] Cyprian advises, "Therefore, dearly beloved

Brother, take heed that the undisciplined be not consumed and perish, that you rule the brotherhood as far as possible with salutary counsels, and that you counsel each one for his salvation."[6] Chrysostom saw shepherding as an awesome responsibility. He made sure that the limits of the shepherding metaphor were not ignored:

> You cannot treat human beings with the same authority with which the shepherd treats a sheep. Here too it is possible to bind and to forbid food and to apply cautery and the knife, but the decision to receive treatment does not lie with the one who administers the medicine but actually with the patient.[7]

The need for preparation for pastoral work is seen in the writings of Origen and Tertullian. Origen compared priests studying secular subjects to the spoiling of the Egyptians by the Israelites. Tertullian did appreciate the need for secular scholarship for polemic reasons, but he cautioned against uncritical reliance on secular knowledge for the work of the ministry. "What indeed has Athens to do with Jerusalem? What concord is there between the Academy and the Church? What between heretics and the Christians?" he asked.

Ministerial self-awareness and congruence were important to early fathers. "You cannot put straight in others what is warped in yourself," said Athanasius. Black Moses, a third-century African ascetic, said: "If a man's deeds are not in harmony with his prayer, he labors in vain."

Pastoral ministry in the early Church gave priority to the resources of the Church, such as the Word, prayer, and sacraments. The Word of God was considered to be central to the care of souls. Pastoral prayer and the sacraments of baptism and communion also served as noble instruments of care.

Teaching was an important ministry in the early Church, as Church leaders assumed that through teaching the Word, one could guide souls toward higher levels of virtue. Clement of Alexandria and Athanasius wrote on the pedagogical aspects of ministry, considering Jesus as their model teacher. They noted that He also embodied His own teachings.

The community of faith continued to be an important resource in the care of souls. The Church as the body of Christ served as the context for caregiving, but it also participated in that ministry. In addition to being the sacramental community of healing, the congregation became a provider of care by financially supporting the needy as well as the priestly caregivers.

Reconciliation was a major theme of ministerial work in the early Church. Polycarp, Bishop of Smyrna, wrote about his approach to dealing with fallen clergy: "You have to restore them, like parts of your own person that are ailing and going wrong, so that the whole body can be maintained in health." The ministry of reconciliation also incorporated counseling as a major aspect of shepherding in the early church. Caregivers considered empathy to be a very important ingredient of good soul care.

Early writings conceptualized the counselor in the following capacities. The caregiver was a physician bringing healing to hurting people, and a guide to those on a spiritual journey. He set people free from bondages and taught them like a faithful educator.

The Church fathers wrote about the methodological issues of pastoral counseling, which are still relevant today. They paid attention to the importance of silence, the use of lanuage, and the reading of body language. For them, counseling was not value-neutral; pastors were expected to give moral counseling. The scripture provided them with moral guidance. These writers also emphasized the importance of using one's words wisely, paying particular attention to the use of language in counseling and ministry. The work of the ministry required spiritual discernment, which meant that caregivers had to be open to the Spirit and the Word to exercise appropriate wisdom in their work. Scriptural counsel had to be given with spiritual discernment.

According to Thomas Oden, the artificial separation of psychology, ethics, and theology did not exist in classical pastoral care. The early Church acknowledged the tension between guilt and forgiveness, grace and effort, discipline and freedom, and Law and Gospel. They maintained a balance between the sternness of the Law and the mercy of the Gospel.

Crisis ministries were also part of classical pastoral work. Many classical writers discussed the importance and methodologies of crisis intervention, with special emphasis on the care of the sick. The Church made a particular effort to offer the ministries of the Church to the seriously sick and dying. Early pastoral writers discussed the subject of suffering in detail, as pastoral work required an honest encounter with this issue. These writers struggled with the issue of theodicy. The connection between evil and suffering was of considerable interest to them. They gave careful attention to the care of the poor and widowed, providing special instructions regarding the obligations of the Church to the poor and needy. The care of the poor involved more than just offering pastoral support; it also included the offering of food, drink, shelter, and clothing.

Classical pastoral writers did not neglect the process and meaning of death in their writing. They explained how to prepare people for dying, and how to minister to those who are left behind. Christian hope is at the center of such ministry.

Middle Ages and Pre-Reformation Period

Although the Charismatic tradition was often seen as part of various heresies throughout history, Eddie Hyatt has traced the history of the Church through the "Dark Ages" to show that a Charismatic tradition survived in spite of suppression and persecution.[8]

Although the Church of the Middle Ages became corrupt in many ways, pastoral care flourished during this period in the form of spiritual direction, especially in the monastic tradition. A more biblical and classical model of pastoral care took place among the Cathari (ca. 1050), Albigenses (ca. 1140), and Waldenses. The theological positions held by pre-Reformation reformers like John Wycliffe (1324-1384), John Huss (1373-1415), and William Tyndale (1494-1536) played an important role in keeping ministry biblical, as opposed to papal.

The Reformers

The Reformation brought the primacy of the Word of God back to Christian ministry. Preaching the Word became the priority of the minister, but pastoral care was also a major concern. Martin Luther, John Calvin, and Ulrich Zwingli particularly emphasized the importance of the pastoral task of caregiving. Luther wrote about the importance of soul care and of the preparation required of ministers who desired to do it:

> Therefore I admonish you, especially those of you who are to become instructors of consciences, as well as each of you individually, that you exercise yourselves by study, by reading, by meditation,

and by prayer, so that in temptation you will be able to instruct consciences, both your own and others', console them, and take them from the Law to grace, from active righteousness to passive righteousness, in short, from Moses to Christ.[9]

Although Luther believed in the priesthood of all believers, he held the pastoral office at a more distinctive level. He considered the scriptures to be the best textbook for pastors. Concerning the writings of the fathers, Luther said:

We are like men who study the sign-posts and never travel the road. The dear fathers wished, by their writings, to lead us to the Scriptures, but we so use them as to be led away from the Scriptures, though the Scriptures alone are our vineyard in which we ought all to work and toil.[10]

Luther, "put great emphasis on pastoral care, which always related directly to the ministry of the Word."[11] Luther believed in an incarnational approach to pastoral ministry. "When Christ wished to attract and instruct men," Luther said, "He had to become a man. If we are to attract and instruct children, we must become children with them."[12] Luther also believed in unconditional love as a condition for helping relationships. He believed that "there is no person on earth so bad that he does not have something about him that is praiseworthy."[13] For Luther, pastoral work involved much more than preaching and teaching; it involved nurturing.

Therefore, something more than merely preaching the Law is required, that a man may also know how he may be enabled to keep it. Otherwise what good does it do to preach that Moses and the Law merely say: This thou shalt do; this God requires of thee. Yes, my dear Moses, I hear what you say; and it is no doubt right and true. But do tell me where am I to get the ability to do what I have unfortunately not done and cannot do.[14]

Soul care must involve enabling people to live the Christian life in a practical way. Anyone can share with others what they "ought" to be doing, but it takes a caring pastor to help people live a virtuous life.

Luther understood the importance of having a theology of suffering; his own theology was built on Christian hope. He believed that "whatever hurts and distresses us does not happen to hurt or harm us but is for our good and profit. We must compare this to the work of the vinedresser who hoes and cultivates his vine."[15]

Calvin believed that the ministry of a pastor involved proclaiming the Word, instructing, admonishing, exhorting privately and publicly, censuring, and enjoining "brotherly corrections." Obviously, pastoral care and counseling were important aspects of ministry as Calvin envisioned it. He believed that the pastor must do preaching, governing, and pastoring. "A pastor needs two voices," he said, "one for gathering the sheep and the other for driving away wolves and thieves. The Scripture supplies him with the means for doing both."[16] Calvin saw the ministry of caring as an aspect of the ministry of *diakonia* or service. The thrust of this ministry involved caring for the poor and the sick.

Martin Bucer (1491-1551) was a disciple of Luther and a teacher of Calvin. According to Switzinger, he identified four duties of the pastor: (1) teach Holy Scriptures, (2) administer sacraments, (3) participate in the discipline of the church, and (4) care for the needy.

Post-Reformation Period

The concept of ministry that the reformers envisioned continued in the post-Reformation Church. Puritan pastors, for instance, were to be preachers and caregivers. They were expected to live a godly life and deliver the message of reconciliation to man. Puritans saw the minister as a "double interpreter", interpreting God to man and interpreting man to God.

Winthrop S. Hudson described the state of the ministry during the Puritan era. While preaching was considered the most important pastoral act, pastoral care was considered essential. The pastoral duties of ministers were well defined: "These were the major facets of the minister's pastoral duties— catechizing, visiting, disciplining, and counseling the members of his flock."[17] Visitation was seen as a very important pastoral duty, so that people would be prepared for a "fruitful life or a happy death." In fact, the pastoral visit was "regarded as a doubly important adjunct because the proper ordering of family life was a major disciplinary concern."[18]

Pastoral counseling was also of great concern to the Puritan pastor. According to Hudson, "pastoral counseling was everywhere regarded as one of the most important as well as the most difficult of the pastoral duties."[19] Clergy were highly encouraged to qualify themselves to be good counselors, because it was well recognized that unskilled counselors could aggravate the "griefs and perplexities" people experienced. Many manuals were produced to help pastors deal with difficult cases. Situations involving moral perplexities in relation to family life, economic activities, political issues, and employment-related problems were common. Jonathan Edwards (1703-1758) and other famous pastors of the eighteenth century saw themselves as people charged with the proclamation of the Gospel and the care of the saints' souls. Ministry involved honoring God and saving men, and saving men involved serving them in the Name of Christ.

John Wesley (1703-1791) was concerned about the salvation, spiritual growth, and nurture of individuals. He is associated with the doctrine of Christian perfection. William Salsbery states that the ministry of pastoral care experienced a renewal under Wesley's ministry, as it "was structured within a biblical framework."[20] In this framework, he found a rationale for developing lay shepherds. Wesley conceptualized a lay preacher/pastor as a gifted person called by God to be trained and sent. The lay leaders taught and cared for their classes, but each leader was under the supervision of Wesley. The lay pastor was expected to see each person in the class once a week and meet with the minister and the stewards of the society once a week.

The nineteenth century provided a good number of faithful ministers. Charles Spurgeon (1834-1892), although he was mostly known for his preaching, was a great pastor. He had a clear understanding of the purpose of ministry. Other great nineteenth-century pastors include Charles Bridges (1794-1869) and G. Campbell Morgan (1863-1945). The modern Pentecostal movement was not born in a theological vacuum. Pentecostal ministry had good models to follow, even though it initially rebounded from them.

A THEMATIC HISTORY

Jaekle and Clebsch, in their classic work *Pastoral Care in Historical Perspective*[21], offer the best thematic history of pastoral care. They found that certain theological themes relating to pastoral care dominated particular historical periods. These themes express the thrust of ministry during these periods.

Sustaining was the pastoral care theme in the early church. The apostles shared the Word, the deacons served the tables, and the practitioners of ministry were acknowledged as gifted people during this period.

The period they designated as the post-apostolic era embodied the theme of *reconciliation* (A.D. 18-306). Pastoral care primarily involved reconciling troubled persons to God. The functional role of the pastor emerged during this period, when ministers began to receive pay for their services.

The theme of the fourth-century church, according to Jaekle and Clebsch, was *guidance*. Pastoral care then involved helping people live in accordance with well-defined Christian culture. The pastoral caregiver was to guide people out of secularism and non-Christian activities into Christian activities. Guidance continued to be the theme of pastoral care during the Dark Ages (A.D. 500-1400). However, as monasticism increased, the monks became interpreters of life. They identified seven deadly sins, and defined a twelve-step ladder of humility.

Healing became the theme of pastoral care for Medieval Christianity (1400-1550). A sacramental system was developed to address the maladies of life, including a sophisticated sacramental system of symbols: Its goal was to restore spiritual and physical health. There was much concern about the activities of demons, as caregivers wanted to provide power for living the Christian life.

Post-Reformation pastoral care (1550-1700) once again embraced the theme of *reconciliation*. Individuals needed reconciliation with God, as well as internal and external disciplines to live righteous lives. The pastor was able to offer confessional forgiveness, but the Church believed that pastors required special training.

During the Enlightenment (1700-1850) the Church shifted its focus of care to *sustaining* and preserving faith. John Bunyan's *Pilgrim's Progress* was written during this period.

As evangelism and discipleship became the important issues of the Missionary Era (1850-1907), *guiding* and *healing* emerged as the themes of pastoral care. The establishment of hospitals and the YMCA, as well as the birth of the Salvation Army, became expressions of this emphasis. The themes of *reconciling* and *sustaining* once again predominated during the Revival period (1908-1919), as World War I caused great need in the Western population.

The next period (1920-1945), which witnessed the Japanese occupation and World War II, initiated a time of *healing* and *sustaining*. Nationalism was incorporated into the ministry, while the emphasis of the Church became eschatological. During this time, the Church needed to be concerned about its own survival.

Jaekle and Clebsch consider the period during the Korean War, between 1945 and 1953, the dark age of the modern Church. As a result of the war, pastoral care focused on *sustaining* the Church, and the following period was a time of rebuilding the Church, with an emphasis on *guiding*. During the sixties, the Church continued its ministry of *sustaining* and *guiding*, while the seventies became a period of mass evangelism and a theme of *reconciliation*.

Jaekle and Clebsch describe *healing* as the main goal of pastoral care. They consider Christian education and preservation of traditions as defining the ministry of *sustaining*, whereas *guiding* involved devotional life, spiritual direction, leadership training, and discipleship. According to these authors, *reconciliation* dealt with evangelism and the issues of social structure.

MINISTRY IN AMERICA

Sydney Mead focuses on the history of pastoral ministry in America, stating that the concept of ministry among the American Evangelicals underwent considerable change during the early history of Protestantism (1607-1850) in America. Perhaps the greatest change was the loss of the priestly function of ministry. "It is obvious that within this broad context the conception of the minister practically lost its priestly dimension as traditionally conceived and became that of a consecrated functionary, called of God, who directed the purposive activities of the visible church."[22] Ministers primarily worked at the conversion of souls; the work of a minister was judged essentially by his success in this area and the pastor's caregiving and nurturing skills became secondary. According to Mead, "When pietistic sentiments and revivalist techniques swept to the crest of evangelicalism in America, the conversion of souls tended to crowd out other aspects of ministers' work."[23]

The second half of the nineteenth century turned out to be a time of significant positive change for American ministry. Faced with industrialization, urbanization, and the challenges of atheism and Darwinism, the Church had to pay special attention to the spiritual needs of people. Although the preaching of the Word still took priority, Christian education and pastoral care also received considerable attention during this period (1850-1950). According to Robert Michaelsen,

> Protestant ministers have carried on a quietly effective work over the years as pastors, as comforters of the sick, the distressed and the bereaved, as counselors of the perplexed, as guides and guardians to those seeking spiritual light and moral rectitude. But we have seen in the last half-century (1900-1950) an increasing awareness of the importance of the minister as pastor.[24]

Seminary curriculum began to particularly emphasize systematic training in pastoral care during this period. The clinical training movement was born as a reaction to traditional theological training, which was not preparing ministers to deal with the personalities and struggles of people.

Twentieth-Century Pentecostal Ministry
The dawn of the twentieth century witnessed the birth of the modern Pentecostal movement. Tracing its American roots to a Bible College in Topeka, Kansas, this movement spread to Houston, to Azusa Street in Los Angeles, and eventually to the entire world. [Some segments of modern Pentecostal movements, such as the 1905 revival at Mukti Mission of Pandita Ramabai in India, cannot be directly connected to Topeka.] The spread of Pentecostalism had an impact on Protestant ministry, as Pentecostals began to emphasize speaking in tongues and divine healing in their churches. They also emphasized evangelism and leading people to the baptism of the Holy Spirit. Pentecostal pastors became involved in the ministry of divine healing.

In spite of their interest in divine healing, the Pentecostals were also more concerned about the saving of souls than the care of souls. Early classical Pentecostals, followed by Charismatics and the subsequent "Third-Wavers," kept the same emphasis. While divine healing was a theological characteristic of the Pentecostals, the denominational and independent Charismatics emphasized healing as a major ministry theme. Although healing was a pastoral theme among all Full Gospel believers, the method of ministry used was often evangelistic rather than pastoral.

It would appear that three unique circumstances initially kept Pentecostals from developing in the area of pastoral care. First, the Charismatic aspect of their worship meant that ministry often took place in the sanctuary. The Holy Spirit did the ministry, so the pastors' skills in this area were not a matter of great concern. The second issue was the puritanical holiness to which most Pentecostals were committed. This meant that many issues requiring pastoral care were seen instead as disciplinary issues. Concern for the individual experiencing the emotional aftermath of divorce, for example, was less important than the issue of disciplining the divorced person and preventing more divorces from occurring. For Pentecostals, caregiving was not the priority in such a situation. Third, Pentecostals were committed to eschatological evangelism. This position encouraged evangelism at all costs, on all occasions. A funeral was not necessarily a place to minister to the grieving and bereaved; the primary objective was to utilize the funeral as an opportunity to win the lost souls who would be attending the service. Pentecostals considered that Jesus might come at any time, and they did not want to leave anyone unsaved.

Pastoral ministry among Charismatics varied among different groups of Charismatic believers. Mainline pastors who were Charismatic were generally trained in pastoral ministry, whereas independent Charismatics typically preferred the evangelistic healing approach. Megachurches among Charismatics were focused on sanctuary ministry. Thankfully, this trend is currently changing, and Spirit-led churches are offering more Christian education and pastoral care.

Pentecostal/Charismatic Bible colleges and theological seminaries have done much to enhance the quality of ministry in full Gospel churches. Four major seminaries have contributed greatly to enhancing ministry in Pentecostal/Charismatic circles. These are Oral Roberts University School of Theology and Missions, the Assemblies of God Theological Seminary, the Church of God School of Theology, and Regent University School of Divinity.

I will conclude this section with a list of various models of pastoral ministry and their proponents, compiled by a student of mine. Gyle Smith was a seminarian at Oral Roberts University, who compiled this list during the fall semester, 1996.

Pastoral Ministry Models
1. Pastor as an example (Richard Baxter).
2. Pastor as a shepherd (Charles Jefferson).
3. Pastor as a parent (Howard Clinebell).
4. Pastor as a keeper of traditions (Thomas Oden).
5. Pastor as a bearer and mediator (Edward Thurneysen).
6. Pastor as a wounded healer (Henri Nouwen).
7. Pastor as a friend (Henri Nouwen).
8. Pastor as a diagnostician (Paul Pruyser).
9. Pastor as the representation of incarnational attitudes (Charles Kemp).
10. Pastor as a servant (Paul Hanson).

11. Pastor as an integrated person (Charles Rassieur).
12. Pastor as an imitator of Christ (Andrew W. Blackwood).

MINISTRY AND DOMINANT SOCIAL CHARACTERS

It has been pointed out that ministry in America has often adopted models that are based on dominant contemporary social characters.[25] For instance, during the seventeenth and eighteenth centuries the educated master was the dominant social character; consequently, ministry adopted this model for itself. The master was an authoritative teacher who had something to say. He was a person formed by learning, and his authority was based on literature and learning. As a learned person, the master was expected to give intellectual leadership. He was considered "holy" due to his study of text.

In the nineteenth century, social change in the United States involved issues of pluralism and church-state relationships. At this time a different type of leadership was needed; society replaced the character of master with that of orator, so that oration replaced teaching. The church adopted this social model in turn, and produced "princes of the pulpit." The dominant ministry model became revivalist or pulpiteer. These individuals preached, thousands flocked to hear them as a form of dramatic or philosophical entertainment, and sinners were saved. They also founded congregations and built buildings to accommodate the growing churches. Regional groups were organized to manage the increased membership, and they devised plans to educate the masses of new church members.

The late nineteenth century and early twentieth century marked an increase in America's belief in science and technology. During this time the concept of profession emerged, and was adopted first by the fields of engineering and medicine. Professionals applied theory to solve problems. The church also adopted the professional model of ministry, and the minister became a builder, organizer, and motivator. Subsequently, ministers began to receive professional training in university settings.

The mission of the church became unclear in the 1930s and 1940s. According to Niebuhr, there was no single model of ministry during this period.[26] General optimism predominated regarding ecumenical theology. The minister functioned as pastoral director during this period. The pastoral director was similar but not identical to the builder. The builder built for the people brought in by the revivalist, while the director maintained institutions already built by others. The roles of preacher, teacher, and priest diminished, while the roles of manager and counselor increased. During the 1960s, the dominant social character was the manager/therapist; as a result, the church adopted the manager/therapist model of ministry. The 1960s also marked a period of confusion about the theological foundations of ministry. What the manager did for the organization, namely solving internal problems, the therapist did for the individual. The minister functioned as organizational problem solver (therapist) as well as counselor of church members.

I attended a seminary during the early 1970s. During that period, counseling and clinical pastoral education were the major emphases in theological education.

At the current time, no one has yet defined the dominant social character of the 1980s and 1990s. In retrospect, this was a period of major development in technology, multimedia, and communications. One could assert that media personalities and corporate executives were the dominant social characters during this period. Similarly, one could argue that ministry adopted these models. The popularity of megachurch ministries, as well as television and multimedia ministries, supports this perspective.

    The preceding review of the changing dominant social figures demonstrates that the Church was often influenced more by society than by its own biblical declarations. Although these adaptations were not necessarily wrong, I feel it is necessary to mention that we have often been more easily influenced by current culture than by God's Word. My hope is that ministry in the twenty-first century will be influenced more by the directives of the Scripture than by the newly emerging dominant social characters.

CHAPTER 3

CHALLENGES OF THE NEW CENTURY

༺✥༻

CONTEMPORARY IMAGES OF MINISTRY

According to Donald E. Messer, ministry today suffers from being perceived through stereotypical images.[1] He believes that many people consider ministers either hired hands or superhuman saints. These images distort the true meaning of ministry as a gift of God to all God's people, because ministry is God's mystery. Messer points out the following contemporary images of ministry:
1. Minister as wounded healer in the community of the compassionate. In this view, the church is the compassionate community and the minister brings healing to others as a wounded person on his own journey toward wholeness.
2. Minister as servant leader in a servant church. Here the church is a community of servants and ministers are servant-leaders.
3. Minister as political mystic in a prophetic community. This view sees the church as a community called to speak prophetically to the

world and ministers are political mystics who do not conform to the world and its systems.
4. Minister as enslaved liberator of the rainbow church. The church in this view is a multicultural global community which stands for liberation of all people from all forms— social, political, economic, etc.— of enslavement. Ministers are liberators who are themselves slaves (servants) of Christ.
5. Minister as practical theologian in a post-denominational church. The church here is not only nondenominational, it is a post-denominational community of faith. Ministers are practical theologians who empower lay leaders to do the work of the ministry.
6. Minister as good shepherd in a global village. The world has become a global village; the church is the flock of God. Ministers are shepherds who feed and lead the sheep.

According to William Willimon, contemporary images of ministry include the following:

1. Minister as media personality.
2. Minister as political negotiator.
3. Minister as therapist.
4. Minister as manager.
5. Minister as resident activist.
6. Minister as preacher.
7. Minister as servant leader.[2]

Willimon proposes that ministry's guiding images should be as follows:

1. Ministry should be countercultural, since according to the scripture, ministers are aliens and exiles (1 Pet. 2:11).
2. Ministry should recover its classical forms of preaching, teaching, evangelizing, and healing.
3. Ministry should be based on critical assessment of the needs of the church and the world.

Willimon sees ministry as an act of God and of the Church. He believes that to be a pastor is to be intimately connected to the Church; thus, ministry is a difficult vocation. Willimon defines ordination as an act of Christ and His Church, for service to Christ and His Church. According to him, ordination arises from above "as a gift of the Holy Spirit" (2 Tim. 1:6). It also arises from below, from the Church's need for leadership. The process of ordination forms those who are to serve as priests for their position within a community of priests. It sets those apart who are to serve as examples. Ordination is an act of collegiality, effected through the laying on of hands (1 Cor. 3:5-9).

CULTURAL CHALLENGES

Someone has compiled the following list of top stories of the last century, in the major fields of life:
War— Hiroshima and Pearl Harbor
Technology— Wright Brothers and Moon Landing
Medicine— Penicillin, Vaccines, and Genetics
Economics— Major Crash and Great Boom
Civil Right— Women's Rights and Civil Rights

Missing from this secular list is the area of religion. One could assert that the top story in this area should be the explosive growth of the Pentecostal/Charismatic movement.

The following predictions have been made for the new century:
1. Technology will transform life as we know it.
2. The United States will have a new face due to increased immigration from nonwhite countries.
3. Medicine will create many moral dilemmas.
4. Education will become an issue for the American Association of Retired Persons.
5. Spirituality will become more important.
6. Post-denominationalism will prevail.

Sociologists and theologians agree that the new century will bring great changes to our lives. How will ministry adjust to this changing world?

Leith Anderson, in his book *Dying for Change,* describes the challenges that faced the American church as it anticipated the twenty-first century.[3] The church today needs to understand these trends and deal with them, if it is to be effective. I have summarized Anderson's observations below:

1. Mobility

People are very mobile today; families do not stay in one place for long, which affects the depth of human relationships. Church membership is not a lifetime commitment.

2. Coloring

Immigration is drastically changing the national demographics. A decreasing Caucasian population, as well as increasing birthrates in minority communities, is changing the color of America.

3. Graying
The number of individuals in America over the age of 65 is expected to increase significantly in the next four decades. The aging baby boomers will hold increasing economic and political power, which will affect everything from education to ministry.

4. Women
The number of women in the workforce is expected to increase significantly. This will leave fewer women to volunteer in the churches and will impact the way the church staffs itself.

5. Pluralism
As an increasingly pluralistic society, modern day America believes in moral relativism. Tolerance is the highest virtue of this postmodern society, which tolerates all sorts of ideologies. This context will challenge modern preachers of the Gospel.

6. Shifts in Segmentation
The traditional economic segmentation of society into lower, middle, and upper classes has been augmented. Societal structure is now determined more by age, gender, race, education, income, marital status, and ethnic background. A church's "fit" for an individual is more important than its geographic location.

7. Short-Term Commitments
Whether they are Sunday school teachers or board members, people are reluctant to make long-term commitments. They prefer task force assignments to long-term appointments, because they are unwilling to do anything that would hinder their personal freedom and self-fulfillment.

8. Decline in the Work Ethic

The goal of "making money" has replaced "developing a meaningful philosophy of life" as the primary objective of the average college freshman. Job fulfillment causes greater concern today than job security and material success is more important than serving others.

9. Conservatism

Younger Americans are more politically conservative than their parents, but they may be more liberal in their morals. Even religious conservatives can be politically liberal. Moral relativism and social pluralism have created a generation without a wholesome worldview.

10. Cocooning

The home is the center of one's personal universe. People prefer home entertainment and home based exercise equipment; the trend of shopping by telephone and the internet is also on the increase. While this may reflect a higher priority on family life, it may also demonstrate a lack of concern for those outside of the family. The activities of the church must compete with family activities; thus evangelism needs to consider privacy issues.

George Barna identified the top "illnesses" found in the church. These issues point to the need for change. They are summarized by Tom Winfield as follows:[4]

1. Pastors are ill-equipped by seminaries. Ministers are trained to preach, teach, and counsel, and then they are asked to run a (church) business. They receive little training in the practical, business, and relationship dimensions of ministry.
2. There is a lack of capable lay leaders to push the church forward. Few Christians feel adept at

evangelism, and those who serve the church leave because they do not get the support they need.
3. Churches spend five times the amount of money on buildings and maintenance as they do on promoting and doing evangelism.
4. Christians, as a whole, fail to hold each other accountable.
5. Christians have not targeted special audiences with personalized messages.
6. Schisms between fundamentalists, evangelicals, and Charismatics, and the battles between mainline denominations and independents, increase.

According to Leith Anderson, the church responds to these challenges in multiple ways:

1. Resistant Church
This church is not open to change. It may have moral, biblical, or institutional reasons for resisting change.

2. Yesterday's Church
This church keeps hoping for yesterday to return tomorrow. Members of this church live in the present during the week and in the past during the weekend.

3. Try Harder Church
This church does what it did yesterday with more effort today. Members of this church do not wish to change yesterday's methods to meet today's challenges; they believe that yesterday's methods will work if more people get involved in them.

4. Surrender Church
   This is the church that has lost its purpose for existence. Realizing that it is unable to change, this church chooses to maintain itself until death.

5. Entrepreneurial Church
   An entrepreneurial leader who is willing to take risks starts this type of church. It is not tied to the past or to tradition, which can be its greatest weakness. It has a marketing and consumer orientation. As retention of members is its main focus, this church can end up in biblical compromise and heresy.

6. Renewing Church
   This church sees value in both tradition and progress. It remains true to both divine revelation and social relevance. This church considers both theology and sociology in its concern for the world around it and has a strategy to reach that world with the good news. The renewing church is also willing to modify its methods to reach its goals.[5]

EXEGETING THE WORLD

Ministers are used to exegeting the Word of God. Exegesis brings out the truth within the sacred text, which needs to be proclaimed in preaching. A successful minister must also exegete the *world* in which ministry takes place. The challenge of ministry is to apply the Word appropriately to the world, which requires that the minister understand his or her context.

David Fisher, in *The 21st Century Pastor,* presents a description of the world in which we are called to minister.[6] I have summarized his observations from my personal perspective:

a. Internationalization
The world has become a global village. Even small towns have people from all over the world. Affordable travel and mass communication have brought the world together in unprecedented ways, so that homogeneous communities no longer exist.

b. Urbanization
The end of the twentieth century witnessed the moving of most of the world's population toward urban centers. People began to leave villages and countrysides, hoping for a better life in the cities. This massive move of people into the large urban centers of the world has changed life in the villages and the cities. Urban centers have become havens for the unemployed and the ambitious, while the resulting urbanization has produced vast problems of sanitation, health care, and crime. From Bombay to Mexico City, nations are struggling with serious human and ecological challenges brought about by urbanization.

c. Secularization
We live in a secular world. While extreme elements of religion are creating havoc, the average person lives in a secular environment. Some claim to be living in a post-Christian era, and postmodernism is making a religion out of secular life. Historic religions have lost their influence upon people and their values.

d. Technology
Modern society is defined by the high-tech industry. While technology has brought individuals and communities together in many ways, it has also caused new alienation between individuals and peoples. Today there are technological "haves" and "have-nots." Although many emphasize

the need for high touch to compensate for the high tech, in effect, technology has increased alienation within our society.

e. Individualism

Our current culture venerates individualism. We do not live in a community of people, but among a collection of individuals. Even in church circles, the community aspect is not often given priority. We have become an egalitarian assembly of self-actualizers, as opposed to a caring community of committed and concerned people. This overemphasis on the individual and his or her fulfillment is a great challenge to a Christian ministry that seeks to foster healthy communities.

f. Materialism/Consumerism

The generation that enjoyed the materialistic blessings of the twentieth century has become a consumer society. Even churches and schools are forced to discuss customer service. Many equate church with Wal-Mart in their expectation of goods and services. They expect spiritual "goods" to be made available in a user friendly manner. Meanwhile, spiritual values are diminishing, only to be replaced by materialism and secular values. Churches and ministries are forced to deal with the consumer mentality.

g. Rootlessness

As people constantly relocate for education and jobs, society becomes increasingly mobile. The nuclear family is continuously under stress from this escalating mobility; grandchildren have less access to their grandparents, and parents are often forced to be away from children. The resulting sense of rootlessness erodes deeper relationships and hinders sustained engagement between individuals.

h. Moral Breakdown

A society that is strictly secularized, highly individualistic, and isolated by technology does not have the grounding for moral development. When individual fulfillment is the ultimate goal, morality becomes relative. This breakdown has not only affected people on Main Street USA, but also those in the highest offices in the land. Corporations crumble due to unethical conduct among their officers, and leaders lacking moral authority paralyze governments. Even the Church has not been exempt from public displays of moral breakdown.

i. Cultural War

America is no longer a melting pot; multiculturalism is the order of the day. While immigrants historically adapted themselves to the American way in their pursuit of the American dream, new immigrants keep their ethnic cultures fully intact with encouragement of the dominant culture. These new immigrants are able to maintain contact with the old country through internet and satellite communication, and can even import native food and clothing. As a result of these amenities and the extreme form of political correctness that exists in America, immigrants have no desire to melt into the mainstream of American society. The outcome is a brewing cultural war. There are tensions between blacks and Asians, Hispanics and Anglos, and a number of other subgroups on issues such as bilingualism, multiculturalism, welfare reform, affirmative action, and a host of other issues.

j. Low Quality of Life

While we have made much progress economically, the general quality of life has gone down in America. Social issues of great magnitude have always existed, but one can easily notice a decline in the quality of human life in today's society. Recent news headlines are shocking: teachers molest their students, parents abuse their children, neighbors abduct neighbors' children, snipers terrorize communities, a president faces impeachment, and clergy are convicted of pedophilia. There is no question that serious flaws exist in the American dream. Effective ministry must understand these dynamics and rise above the issues to bring about spiritual interventions. The twenty-first century demands the intervention of the Kingdom of God in all its affairs.

Fisher points out additional challenges facing ministry today. For instance, today's culture is an authority-resistant culture. The baby boomer generation, which has always been suspicious of authority, now dominates modern society. Today's Church is also resistant to authority. People expect church to be strictly democratic; as a result, individuals frequently challenge the authority of the Bible and that of bishops and pastors. As the Apostle Paul prophesied, people seem to have itching ears:

> For the time will come when men will not put up with sound doctrine. Instead, to suit their own desires, they will gather around them a great number of teachers to say what their itching ears want to hear. They will turn their ears away from the truth and turn aside to myths (2 Tim. 4:3, 4).

Although these new challenges make effective ministry more difficult, Christians are called to be the light of the world and the salt of the earth. God still loves this world and expects us to bring His message of love and redemption to this generation. We will be able to meet this challenge only as we depend on the power of the Holy Spirit.

DIFFICULTIES IN MINISTRY
John A. Sanford, in *Ministry Burnout*, listed nine difficulties faced by ministers:
1. The job of the ministering person is never finished.
2. The ministering person cannot always tell if his work is having any results.
3. The work of the ministering person is repetitive.
4. The ministering person is constantly dealing with people's expectations, which are often unrealistic.
5. The ministering person must work with the same people year in and year out.
6. Because he works with people in need, there is a particularly great drain on the energy of the ministering person.
7. The ministering person deals with many people who come to him or the church, not for solid spiritual food, but for "strokes."
8. The ministering person must function a great deal of the time in his "persona" (the front we assume in order to meet and relate).
9. The ministering person may become exhausted by failure.[7]

Ministers should take notice of Sanford's observations and make sure that they take preventative measures to enjoy a meaningful ministry that will last a lifetime.

EVANGELISM IN THE NEW AGE
Whether we live in India or America, we do not live in the world in which we were born; in this sense, we are all immigrants. As immigrants, we struggle to adjust to our new world. Born in the age of horse and buggy and steam

engine trains, we now live in the age of supersonic jets and space shuttles. Remember when we had to travel to distant places with some important news? Today, with wireless phones and satellite communication facilities everywhere, people no longer depend on the old ways.

I recall that just decades ago a cable sent from the United States took three days to reach my father in Kerala State, India. Today, instead of sending cables, I dial directly and the phone rings within moments in my father's living room.

SEVEN FORCES

What are the powers that are changing our world? I believe that the following seven forces are shaping the modern world:

1. Science and Technology

The strongest force impacting our world is technology. It has moved us from old typewriters to new computers. Television, cell phones, the internet, and many other inventions have changed our entire way of life. A *National Geographic* reporter described the glowing television sets in the homes of slum-dwelling families in Mumbai, who now have access to more than fifty cable television channels.[8] Technology is enslaving modern man. Whereas children used to play ball outdoors, they now get fat sitting and staring at television screens or computer monitors for hours.

2. Knowledge

Information is the second force shaping today's world. The internet has created an information superhighway. Knowledge is flowing in full color on the internet, allowing one to log on from anywhere and study any subject at any time. Unfortunately, we have increasing knowledge but lack wisdom; we have information, but we do not know how to evaluate it. We lack the skill to discern between what is good and worthwhile, and what is not.

3. Cultural Change and Speed of Life

Our world is changing so fast that people feel like passengers on a roller coaster. Easy access to television and increasing opportunities for world travel are enabling people to incorporate features of foreign cultures into their own. Old preachers in India are clad in suits, while young Americans wear nose rings! Cultural barriers are being removed. Unfortunately, some have adopted all new traditions, while others resist change completely. This has produced cultural clashes all over the world. Violence has become common, "ethnic cleansing" has entered our vocabulary, and time has become a rare commodity. We have instant coffee, instant meetings, and instant weddings!

4. New Spirituality

Fed up with materialism, yet enslaved by it, the world has adopted a new spirituality. This spirituality is defined by the absence of God. Modern man does not believe in God, but in a nebulous spiritual Force. Instead of acknowledging God the Father, God the Son, or God the Holy Spirit, the New Age religion mixes Hinduism, Buddhism, Christianity, and aspects of various primitive religions. Ayurvedam (Eastern medicine) and transcendental meditation are sold as spirituality in America, and even extreme environmentalism has become a religion for some. Today's pseudo spirituality has no Ten Commandments to guide it; it affirms all alternate lifestyles, and tolerance of everything is its highest moral value.

5. Broken Families

Families are breaking down on Main Street, USA. Families, regardless of their race and economic status, are in distress. At one time, Asians could brag about their strong families; even non-Christian Asians had strong family ties. This is not the case anymore; many Asian families are falling apart. Working parents have no time for their children, and the earphones blasting modern music into our youth's brains prevent them from hearing their parents' words even when the family is together.

6. Money is God

The love of money has always existed, but this generation has taken that concept to new heights. Man is willing to do anything for a few dollars. Keeping up with the Joneses requires a lot of borrowing, and many cannot afford to pay back the debts. Some parents have no values to give their children, only falling stocks.

7. Hopelessness

Ours is a hopeless age. There is no cure for AIDS, and heart disease and cancer are still medical challenges. The gap between the rich and the poor is widening. Terrorism has become a global concern. Suicide bombers represent the ultimate hopelessness of our age.

STRATEGIC EVANGELISM

How shall we evangelize the inhabitants of such an age? I believe that our evangelistic efforts must take into account all these forces that are shaping our world. Let me propose some ideas to be included in a strategic plan to evangelize in the twenty-first century.

1. Use Technology
Use technology to spread the Gospel. Since television and the internet are today's marketplaces, we can bring the message of the Gospel to these popular forums as eagerly as we brought it to the marketplace through open-air meetings. We must not compromise the Gospel, but we should be willing to change our evangelistic methods.

2. Increase Education
Train ministers at a higher level. The knowledge level of the population is increasing; consequently, ministers must be given better education for ministry. Bible schools must move beyond being cottage industries. We need Bible schools that can combine academics with spiritual empowerment and practical skills. Pastors need to learn leadership skills and conflict resolution strategies. We must alter the seminary's tendency to produce only teachers, and ensure that theological schools produce practicing pastors and evangelists. Ultimately, we need theological schools that produce apostles, prophets, evangelists, pastors, and teachers (Eph. 4).

3. Design Creative Methods
Offer spiritually refreshing ministry to people living in today's fast-paced society. Hurting people are attracted by a Gospel that heals; therefore, we must design creative ways to draw their attention to the good news.

4. Offer Transformation
Preach the Word and teach biblical spirituality, not just cultural Christianity or insensitive versions of Pentecostalism. Instead of preaching about trends and fashions, we must preach Jesus Christ and Him crucified. Emphasize life transformation rather than religious appearance.

5. Strengthen Families

Attract souls through programs that strengthen marriage and family life. People must be taught how to be good husbands, wives, and parents. Counseling seminars, camp meetings, marriage classes, and parenting seminars, are some of the means by which we can attract people to the Lord Jesus. These programs will also benefit believers.

6. Live the Gospel

Practice lifestyle evangelism. Our lifestyle must reflect our faith, so that our preaching and practice will match. We must live as if Christ is our treasure, not material things. This requires that believers be taught to share material goods with others in need, and learn to give tithes and offerings. Giving is not just for Westerners; all God's people must be givers. For this to happen, pastors must teach the blessings of giving in the name of Jesus. We must have ways and means to assist unbelievers in need.

7. Offer Hope

Be people of hope. In order for unbelievers to see our hope in Christ, we must adopt a lifestyle based on hope. If we allow others to see how we handle disappointments, they will see our hope in the midst of crises. People who watch our lives must see Christ in us, the hope of glory!

NEED FOR TRUE REVIVAL

Reports of revival are emerging from all the continents of the earth. It seems that God is moving by His Spirit in a new way, all over the globe, as the world enters a new century and millennium. History tells us that the beginning of the twentieth century also witnessed a worldwide spiritual awakening. The modern Pentecostal/Charismatic movement is the outgrowth of that revival.

The world has seen many revivals. The day of Pentecost was the beginning of the greatest revival in history. Peter and the other apostles of the Lord Jesus were the human instruments of that divine intervention. Many centuries later, the Reformation became a mighty revival. Individuals such as Luther, Calvin, and Zwingli became the human leaders of that revival. The holiness movement is another example of revival, as is the historic Methodist movement. God used John Wesley and others mightily in that outpouring. Many of us are familiar with the Colonial revival in America and recognize names such as Jonathan Edwards and Charles Finney. The Welsh and Pentecostal revivals, led by Evan Roberts and Charles Parham respectively, are also widely known by believers. Oral Roberts, T.L. Osborn, Kathryn Kuhlman, and others led the Charismatic revival of the 1950s and 60s, with its emphasis on healing. Many of today's revivalists are disciples of these leaders.

It is difficult to name the true leaders of today's revival; leading personalities will emerge over the course of time. Currently, Charismatics consider locations such as Toronto and Pensacola to be centers of revival.

I am sharing a brief history of revivals to encourage Pentecostals and Charismatics to expect a revival. The truth is that we— all of us— need it. Let me explain to you the type of revival I desire.

I long for a revival that embodies the best of all the revivals we have had since Christ. I say this with the knowledge that each revival had a specific emphasis, and that ordering an all-inclusive revival may not be realistic. But as a third-generation minister, I long for a true revival that contains the best of all God has. What are the best qualities of the revivals we have seen and heard about? Let us take a brief look at the ones mentioned above.

The most significant aspect of previous revivals is their emphasis and reliance on the Word of God for authority and guidance. Although people initially questioned the manifestations of these revivals, the revivalists were eventually able to demonstrate the authenticity of what was happening based on the Bible. They did not feel that anything else, including personal experiences, carried more weight than the written Word of God. This is especially true of the modern Pentecostal revival. Although people attacked early Pentecostals concerning the issue of speaking in tongues, the leaders were able to show its authenticity from the Word of God. Dependence on the Word of God helped to establish truth and identify false doctrines.

Second in importance was the concern and caution about counterfeit revivals which the Pentecostals called "wild fire." Godly men and women watched over the people of God to protect them from the enemy's attacks and counterfeits.

Third, there was an emphasis on prayer and brotherly love. During the period of segregation in America, the early Pentecostals practiced racial integration through the Holy Spirit.

Fourth, earlier revivals promoted missionary concerns. People who were touched by the revivals were concerned about the salvation of peoples and nations; as a result, they were willing to go into every person's world with the power of the Gospel. The believers wanted to see signs and wonders promote the Kingdom of God on the earth.

Finally, personal integrity was valued in all previous revivals. People who failed in this area ultimately failed in ministry. We live in a time when people seem to separate performance from character. This may be acceptable in many secular areas, but for the disciples of Jesus, integrity is a requirement. The fruit of the Spirit must be evident in the lives of ministers and people. Lies about oneself or one's ministry were not tolerated in the long run; truth was allowed to prevail, and its natural consequences followed. The revival I desire has the following qualities: I want the Word of God to have the last say on all issues, and I want only the true fire of God, regardless of how attractive or powerful the alternatives might be. I seek a revival that emphasizes prayer and brotherly love. The revival will promote evangelism and missions, and place an emphasis on signs, wonders, miracles, and healings. A revival should bring forth the manifestation of all the gifts of the Spirit, yet it must also incorporate the fruits of the Spirit. Integrity and holy living will characterize all spiritual leaders.

NEED FOR INTEGRITY

A city bribes the Olympic Committee in order to host the winter games, and judges fix the gold medals before the competitions. The leaders of Enron, the country's seventh largest corporation, exploit its employees and investors in scandalous trading practices, and each leader pleads the Fifth Amendment before Congressional committees. Not one businessman in that company stands up and confesses his mistakes or reports that he abstained from the unethical practices. It is undeniable that modern day America lacks integrity. This should concern all citizens, especially those of us who are called to minister to this so-called "post-Christian" society.

Psychologists and theologians concur that integrity is the highest value in an individual's character, and both agree that it is hard to sustain hope in a place without integrity. Erik Erikson, the famous social psychologist, wrote that human life progresses through eight stages. A person faces a crisis at each stage of life; he enjoys health if he overcomes the crisis, and suffers the consequences if he does not. Each crisis, according to Erikson, is an opportunity for growth and development.

The eight crises of life, according to Erikson, are listed below. A healthy person is one who is able to incorporate the positive aspect, such as trust, autonomy, etc. at each stage.
1. Trust vs. Mistrust
2. Autonomy vs. Shame
3. Initiative vs. Guilt
4. Industry vs. Inferiority
5. Identity vs. Identity Confusion
6. Intimacy vs. Isolation
7. Generativity vs. Stagnation
8. Integrity vs. Despair[9]

The final issue in a person's life, according to Erikson, is integrity. Integrity, in Erikson's vocabulary, means hope. Erikson reports that only those who have genuine integrity can live and die in hope. Integrity allows one to speak the truth; it causes one's words and deeds to become congruent, and it promotes love and unselfishness. Integrity makes people trustworthy.

According to the Word of God, all Christians should be living examples of integrity. Unfortunately, integrity is not always evident, even among Christians. What a tragedy! How wonderful it would have been to see one Christian man or woman stand up and admit his or her failure at the Olympics or at Enron. How strange that the Christian community said virtually nothing about these events! Newspaper editors and politicians had more to say about the lack of integrity in these events than American preachers! WWJD— What Would Jesus Do?

The Bible says that our "yes" should mean yes, and our "no" should mean no. The Pharisees were experts in external religion, and Jesus was not soft on them. Believers today still face the same temptation to keep our faith external and our Christian differences superficial.

I am not suggesting that Christians go and overturn the tables of the money changers, but I do believe that the Lord is calling us to be people of integrity. He desires that we practice our faith in all areas of our lives; therefore, it is time that believers examine their own lives. We may not be bribing the Olympic Committee or robbing stockholders and pensioners; nonetheless, we continually face many temptations to violate integrity.

People with integrity do not say one thing and practice another; they do not break their word. People with integrity abstain from character assassination and do not abuse their parishioners.

We *can* model integrity before our neighbors and our children, and we *can* demonstrate that Christ has truly transformed our lives. Our faith is not limited to our conduct within the church; we must embody our faith in community life. A life of faith is a life of integrity; it would be wonderful if Christians could be known as doers of the Word rather than preachers of the same.

PROBLEM OF DENIAL

I clearly recall the day that my daughter's old red car was legally parked on the road in front of our house, plainly visible in the early morning light from both ends of our quiet neighborhood street. Apparently the young lady in the white sedan was not paying attention to her surroundings, because she hit the empty red car from behind and caused serious damage.

My neighbors heard the crash and looked out of their windows in disbelief. As we came out of our house, the young woman in the white New Yorker parked her car and walked toward us amidst the scattered debris. We were in shock. The driver approached us and explained that she had been rushing in order to open the restaurant where she worked. Her hands were shaking as she apologetically gave us her driver's license and insurance papers. Although I was very upset, I felt sorry for the young woman, who reminded me of my own kids.

The New Yorker had also sustained significant damage, but was still running. By the time I began to take down the insurance information, the young lady, who was cursing herself for the accident, noticed that our car was not roadworthy and that my daughter would need a ride. Seeing our predicament, she said, "Tell me where you need to go. I will give you a ride." I was obviously not willing to send my daughter with this stranger who had just caused a massive accident. I politely declined her offer and said, "That's OK. I will take her." To my surprise, the woman was offended when I declined her offer. She yelled, "I will give her a ride. I am no reckless driver!"

The situation was ironic. The young woman stood next to a car which she had just destroyed, arguing with me that she was not a reckless driver! I thought to myself, "You may not be a reckless driver, but I am looking at a wreck that you caused this morning on this empty neighborhood road, and I am not about to trust you with my daughter's life!"

Denial is a major problem for human beings. Psychologists report that we deal with difficult issues, particularly losses, through denial. For instance, when you hear about the death of a friend or loved one, often your first response is, "No, not that person." That is denial, and it is one way human beings cope with loss.

Not all denial is bad. For instance, in the above example the denial serves as a shock absorber. We are able to accept the death, but gradually. If the temporary denial continues and we act as if the event did not happen, then it becomes an unhealthy form of denial.

Individuals, families, and communities all experience problems. The reality of having a problem is less harmful, however, than hiding the problem behind denial for an extended period of time. Families that deal with problems by denying their existence, instead of naming, owning, and solving them, are called dysfunctional families. Although healthy families may also experience problems, generally they face an issue and seek solutions.

Someone once told the story of an elephant sitting in the living room of a house, while family members acted as if it did not exist. Visitors to the home could see the elephant, but the family acted as if they could not see it. Although they were in denial, everything they did was affected by the presence of the elephant and the space it occupied in the house. Problems in families and communities are often like this elephant; even when we deny their existence, they affect us in profound ways.

I have a friend who illustrates this point using the following example. According to my friend, if one person calls you a horse, you should ignore it. If two people call you a horse, you should not mind it. However, if a third person calls you a horse, then you should buy a saddle and put it on your back.

Sometimes one issue about ourselves is brought to our attention again and again, yet we continue to ignore it. This is a form of denial that we would be wise to face directly. If several unrelated people confront you about the same problem they have observed, or if you seem to be continually faced with the same issue, perhaps it is time to take a close look at yourself to determine if you need to make some changes in your life. If you continually hear statements such as, "You talk too much," "You criticize too much," or "You seem hateful," then you should consider a serious self-evaluation.

This also applies to families and communities. If the same comment continually emerges, it may contain some truth that we must seek to address. Denial can only prolong a problem, even for ministers and churches. This applies to all of the issues and challenges facing the church and ministry today that we addressed in this chapter. We cannot ignore these matters; we must begin to respond and make healthy changes.

Change in a person or ministry is not easy. Yet although it may be a fearful process, it is better to make necessary changes, rather than dealing with the conesquences of trying to maintain the status quo. God can help us to make the required changes. As long as we stay in denial, we refuse to accept God's help for us. The best thing we can do is get beyond denial and acknowledge the problems. This process should lead us to seek God's help. While denial does not bring healing, admitting our problems and seeking God's help will.

Christian ministry in the twenty-first century is facing many serious challenges. Acknowledging these challenges does not mean accepting defeat; rather, it allows us to come up with creative ways to address the challenges. We cannot alter the message of Spirit-led ministry, but we must adopt new methods and seek Spiritual power to deliver that message more effectively.

CHAPTER 4

MINISTRY AND THE HOLY SPIRIT

༺༻

Christian ministry is more than just a helping profession; ministers are called by God for His purposes. The most important aspect of ministry is the minister's ongoing relationship with the One who called him. According to Mark, Jesus ordained the twelve that they might be with Him. They were to preach, teach, and bring deliverance to people, but being *with* Jesus was the priority.

Moses' encounter with God at Mt. Horeb gives us a clue to the mystery of God's empowerment for ministry. Moses said to God, "Suppose I go to the Israelites and say to them, 'The God of your fathers has sent me to you,' and they ask me, 'What is his Name?' Then what shall I tell them?" God said to Moses, "I AM WHO I AM. This is what you are to say to the Israelites: 'I AM has sent me to you'" (Exod. 3:13-14). God defines himself as I AM, not I DO. Just as God's work in His universe flows out of His being, a minister's being is also more important than his doing; therefore, what we do must flow out of our being. Our identity is anchored in God and based on His call.

Ministers are always in the process of becoming. Jesus told His disciples that He would make them fishers of men. We are in the process of being made, and the making happens as we follow Christ. God, through His Spirit, is molding us and shaping us; in other words, He is working on our being. The prophet Jeremiah writes about the potter's house and describes how the potter creates a vessel. That creative process is stressful for the vessel, but in order to become a vessel of honor, one must be willing to go through the challenging process. God does the molding and shaping through His Holy Spirit. Authentic Christian ministry is a Spirit-filled, Spirit-led ministry; it is God's work, done by God's Spirit, through the servants who have been molded by His hand.

In spite of all his preparation and training, a minister is completely dependent on the Holy Spirit. A ministry does not belong to the minister; it belongs to Christ. Our skills and resources are necessary, but they are not sufficient. I think of the words of Dean Collin Williams, of Yale Divinity School, who said that the accumulation of all training in ministry equals no more than five loaves of bread. Until those loaves are given to the Master Who will bless them, break them, and multiply them, the disciples cannot feed the multitude. Although ministers may have personal and religious resources, ultimately the presence of God's Spirit makes the difference in their effectiveness. The power of the Spirit is the true dynamic in ministry. "You shall receive power when the Holy Spirit has come upon you" (Acts 1:8, NKJV). Authentic ministry is the result of that process. A ministry without the Holy Spirit is a powerless ministry.

The Apostle Paul exhorted believers, "Be filled with the Spirit" (Eph. 5:18). He knew that by being filled with the

Spirit we would have access to the gifts of the Spirit, and that we would be formed by the fruits of the Spirit.

NOUWEN'S VIEW

Henri Nouwen's book, *The Wounded Healer*, provides a sobering view of ministry.[1] According to Nouwen, a Christian minister is a reflective person— one who reflects theologically on life and life issues. A minister is also active and evocative; he does not wait forever, rather he initiates. To Nouwen, a Christian minister is an individual who has discovered the voice of the Spirit within himself; in other words, he listens to God's voice. A minister is a wounded healer; he is one who knows the pain of being hurt, but also one who is in the process of being made whole. Nouwen believes that as we are healed by Christ's stripes (Isa. 53), God can use our wounds as healing resources for others. According to Nouwen, a minister must care for himself and for others, and he must test everything for biblical authenticity. He is not afraid to die because he is a person of hope. Ultimately, as a person of hope, a Christian minister must also be a person of prayer.

Henri Nouwen's descriptions of ministry, although significant, lack the power dimension of ministry. Certainly, the Gospel of Jesus, as Nouwen presents it, contains the mystery of powerlessness. Jesus was not born in a palace, and He did not choose men of powerful character to be His disciples. Jesus did not possess the political and structural power that was characteristic of authority in His day. But through Christ, God was reconciling the world to Himself. Nouwen is correct when he points out that we often adopt worldly concepts and images of power and overlook the mystery of power through powerlessness, as found in the Kingdom. However, the Kingdom of God, as it manifests in ministry through the power of the Holy Spirit, is also a mystery. God's strength is made perfect in our weaknesses.

SPIRIT-FILLED MINISTRY

God, in Christ, was the Word become flesh (John 1:14). Jesus, the incarnate Word, inaugurated the Kingdom of God. The power of the Kingdom was manifested in Jesus' life and ministry as the Spirit of the Lord rested upon Him. The same power of God's Spirit also manifested as explosive power in the disciples on the day of Pentecost.

Spirit-filled ministry is power-filled ministry. Jesus said, "All authority is given unto me." This authority was also given to His disciples, who were to continue the ministry of Jesus. Scripture states, "These signs will accompany those who believe." Signs, wonders, and miracles are possible today because the same Spirit that raised Jesus from the dead now dwells in us (Rom. 8:11). Jesus instructed us not only to preach and teach, but also to heal. Healing is a sign of the Kingdom of God and a gift of the Holy Spirit. Ministers have the privilege and the authority to pray for healing; whether their ministry is pastoral or evangelistic, a powerful ministry must include healing.

A minister is a person in dialogue. As we have seen, ministry can be defined as being in dialogue with the world and in dialogue with God at the same time; a minister communicates simultaneously with God and man. A Spirit-filled minister is an individual whose being and doing are connected. Consequently, Spirit-filled ministry must balance love for God and man, with power received from God on behalf of man.

Generally speaking, there are two types of ministry. One over-emphasizes love but does not make room for power; the other over-emphasizes power but neglects agape love. A Spirit-filled ministry must maintain equilibrium between these two dimensions of love and power.

The greatest contribution of ministry is hope. Thus, Spirit-filled ministers are called to be hope-bearers. This hope does not pertain primarily to events and dates of the future; rather it reflects a Person. This hope is a Person whose name is Jesus. Ministry is hope bearing because Christ in us is the hope of glory.

Spirit-led ministry begins with a revelation of who Christ is. When Peter was confronted with the question, "Who do you say that I am?" he responded, "You are the Christ, the Son of the living God." Jesus told Peter that it was not flesh and blood that revealed this truth to him; it was His Father in heaven. The Samaritan woman who witnessed to her listeners said, "Come, see a man who told me all things that I ever did. Could this be the Christ?" She was at the verge of a revelation as she encountered the Lord Jesus. "Did not our hearts burn within us?" wondered the disciples who met the risen Lord on the Emmaus road, as they received the revelation of His identity. This was the beginning of the disciples' ministry of proclamation. St. Paul's experience was very similar; he had a sudden revelation of who Jesus was. His response to the encounter with Jesus was, "Who are you, *Lord*?"

Scripture illustrates that Spirit-led ministry involves risks. When Jesus healed the demoniac, the natives asked Jesus to depart from their coast. Stephen, who proclaimed the truth to his countrymen, was stoned to death, and Paul was left for dead outside the city. Spirit-led ministry also requires a willingness to risk one's reputation. Jesus was accused of being a friend of tax collectors, and Paul was called a rioter. In spite of all this, Spirit-led ministry produces results. The blind see, the lame walk, the wind and the waves obey, and legions of evil spirits depart.

Spirit-filled ministry is rewarding. I would be amiss to lead anyone to believe that ministry is only about risk. Ministers are rewarded beyond risks and results. In fact, ministers should not over-emphasize results. We are called to be faithful, not successful, and we are promised eternal rewards for our faithfulness.

A minister's affirmation comes from the call of God, not from the external results of ministry. Jesus did not depend on His ministerial results to give Him affirmation. His Father affirmed Him even before His first public miracle, when God said, "This is my Son, in whom I am well pleased." Depending on results in order to gain affirmation is a roller coaster ride, because results vary in ministry. Days of triumphant entry are often followed by days of sorrow; escaping danger as a fugitive in a basket may follow successful campaigns. Yet God's call and His faithfulness remain unchanging. Our affirmation comes from God who called us.

Spirit-filled ministry is a prayerful ministry. Prayer must always be a part of ministry. The earliest church was involved in "the apostle's doctrines, fellowship, breaking of bread, and prayer." Scripture strongly reinforces the emphasis, indicating that the apostles *devoted* themselves to "prayer and the ministry of the Word." One can feel the human emotion of Ananias through his prayer, as he was instructed to visit the recent convert Saul: "Lord, I have heard many reports about this man." A minister is compelled to pray about everything. This type of constant prayer moves beyond the realm of formal prayer, and is expressed as the cry of one's heart raised toward heaven on behalf of someone or some situation. In prayer, we seek God's will and His Word for every situation.

EMPOWERMENT

Spirit-filled ministry is an empowered ministry. One cannot obtain Kingdom outcomes with one's own personal power; God's work requires God's power. Even the Son of God relied on the power of the Spirit. "The Spirit of the Lord is upon me," Jesus said. He also instructed His disciples to wait in Jerusalem until they received power from heaven. "But you will receive power when the Holy Spirit comes on you and you will be my witnesses in Jerusalem, and in all Judea and Samaria, and to the ends of the earth" (Acts 1:8). Jesus knew that this band of locals could not reach the ends of the earth without the limitless power of the Holy Spirit. On the day of Pentecost, Peter stood up to preach after he received the Holy Spirit. His Spirit-empowered preaching converted three thousand people that day. Ananias told Saul of Tarsus: "Brother Saul, the Lord— Jesus, who appeared to you on the road as you were coming here— has sent me so that you may see again and be filled with the Holy Spirit" (Acts 9:17). Saul needed the power of the Holy Spirit to stand before "the Gentiles and their kings and before the people of Israel" (Acts 9:15).

I have observed the difference between the ministry of highly trained ministers who lack the power of the Holy Spirit, and the ministry of generally unlearned individuals, ministering under the anointing of the Holy Spirit. I must concede that ministry based on training, without the power of the Holy Spirit, is ineffective. Paul's description of "having a form of godliness but denying its power" is only a form. The world needs genuinely Spirit-filled, trained ministry.

Theologians who write about ministry often neglect the subject of Holy Spirit empowerment. Some will mention this issue but will not clarify its meaning. It is high time to declare that Christian ministers must be filled with the Holy Spirit; there is no substitute for this power.

Ministers are equipped to lead the people of God under the power of the Holy Spirit. The power of God will manifest in all aspects of ministry. One can preach, teach, and heal by the power of the Holy Spirit. The power of God will also manifest in signs and wonders. The lame will walk (Acts 3:6-7), prison doors will open (Acts 5:17-19), and the divisions between Jew and Gentile, rich and poor, and all other groups can vanish under the power of the Holy Spirit (Acts 10:44-46). The power of God can deliver the oppressed and set the captives free (Acts 16:18, 26).

AUTHORITY FROM JESUS

Spirit-filled ministry operates in the authority of Jesus, but authentic ministry is often challenged on the basis of its authority. Jesus was questioned many times about His authority. People who knew His background wondered how He dared to do the things He did. They wanted to know who authorized Him. Ministry still faces this challenge in modern society. Spirit-filled ministry claims its authority from Jesus; a minister needs to know the kind of authority Jesus continues to possess today.

Upon entering Jerusalem, Jesus went into the temple and cleansed it. His words and deeds were very assertive, and His entry into Jerusalem stirred the city. People asked, "Who is this?" (Matt. 21:10). On a different occasion, the disciples asked again, "Who is this?" (Luke 8:25). The cleansing of the temple provided an answer to this question in the book of Matthew. Jesus was the one with authority over the temple in order to claim it as a house of prayer; He had more authority than the high priest and the other officers of the temple. Luke, in chapter eight, answers the disciples' question in a similar way. We can summarize the issue as follows.

1. Jesus Has Authority over Natural Forces
While Jesus and the disciples were sailing across the Sea of Galilee, Jesus fell asleep. A great storm arose, which put them in grave danger, so the disciples cried out to Jesus and woke Him up. He rebuked the wind and the waves, and they obeyed Him. Luke testifies of Jesus' authority over natural forces, which even included calming the stormy seas!

2. Jesus Has Authority over Demonic Forces
Luke went on to report the healing of a demon-possessed man in the region of the Gadarenes. This man was living in the tombs, naked and deranged, but when he met Jesus, he fell at His feet. "Jesus asked him, 'What is your name?' 'Legion,' he replied, because many demons had gone into him. And they begged him repeatedly not to order them to go into the Abyss" (Luke 8:30, 31). Jesus gave the demons permission to go into the herd of pigs. The herd rushed into the lake and drowned, but the man who was set free sat at the feet of Jesus "dressed and in his right mind." According to Luke, Jesus has authority over demonic forces. They tremble at His presence and obey Him.

3. Jesus Has Authority over Sickness
Luke reports that upon Jesus' return a great crowd greeted Him and almost crushed Him. A particular woman in that crowd had been suffering from chronic bleeding for twelve years. Physicians could not heal her, and she was desperate. As this nameless woman came up behind Jesus and touched the edge of His garment, she was instantly healed. "Who touched me?" Jesus asked. "Someone touched me; I know that power has gone out of me," He

added. The woman came forward, fell at His feet, and gave her testimony. "Daughter, your faith has healed you. Go in peace" (Luke 8:48). In these passages, Luke presents evidence that Jesus has authority over sickness and even over incurable diseases. I recall the dean of ORU's former School of Medicine, a specialist in infectious diseases, sharing his personal opinion that this woman had a form of cancer. This report would only extend Luke's witness that Jesus has authority over all diseases, including cancer.

4. Jesus Has Authority over Death

The eighth chapter of Luke's Gospel ends with the story of Jesus raising the daughter of a man named Jairus, a synagogue ruler. While Jesus was ministering to the woman in the crowd who had just been healed, word came to Jairus that his beloved daughter was dead. Jesus said to Jairus, "Don't be afraid; just believe, and she will be healed" (Luke 8:50). Jesus went to Jairus' house and raised the twelve year old girl from the dead. "Her spirit returned, and at once she stood up" (Luke 8:55). In this account, Luke presents evidence of Jesus' ultimate authority, which extends even over the last enemy, death.

Matthew concludes his Gospel with the words of Jesus: "All authority in heaven and on earth has been given to me. Therefore go and make disciples of all nations, baptizing them in the name of the Father and of the Son and of the Holy Spirit, and teaching them to obey everything I have commanded you. And surely I am with you always, to the very end of the age" (Matt. 28:18-20). When questioned about authority, this is what a minister needs to remember: Jesus has all authority and He has given it to His disciples who are called to represent His Kingdom. We minister in His name, and He promised His presence as we minister. Therefore, we function in His authority. Spirit-filled ministry requires the authority that comes through the Name of Jesus who called us and set us apart for His service.

THE AUTHORITY OF THE WORD OF GOD

A weakening of the authority of God's Word among Christians has led to weakness in ministry today. We have discussed the minister's authority based on the call of God and based on the Name of Jesus; however, the authority of the Bible as the Word of God is the foundation of any other claims of authority. A Spirit-filled minister must believe that the Bible is the written Word of God, just as Jesus is the living Word of God. Only such a conviction can enable a minister to proclaim the Word of God with authority and power. This is not an easy task in this age of relativism and multiculturalism. The New Age religion considers tolerance to be the highest virtue. Taken to an extreme, this means that all religious books have the same significance and level of authority. A Spirit-filled minister cannot agree with this supposedly "enlightened" position.

God inspired the Bible; it is God-breathed, and it has authority to command our obedience. While the scriptures of other religions have their places in history, as far as a Spirit-filled minister is concerned the Bible holds a unique position as the Word of God. It contains the whole truth and the whole counsel of God.

During my student days many years ago, Howard Ervin, professor of Old Testament at Oral Roberts University, helped my understanding of this issue. He said that we must believe the Bible to be the Word of God for the following reasons:
1) Internal witness: The Bible says that it is the Word of God.
2) Historical witness: The Church has said for two thousand years that the Bible is the Word of God.

3) Personal witness: The Bible has changed my personal life.
4) Existential witness: Preaching and teaching the Bible produces the same results today as it did two thousand year ago.
5) Spiritual witness: The Spirit of God is bearing witness with my spirit that the Bible is the Word of God.

These statements are not proof statements. They do not attempt to say that the Bible is a science or history textbook, although much science and history can be found in the Bible. These five statements support me as I take a step of faith to confess that the Bible is the Word of God, which requires my obedience.

One's convictions regarding the Word of God are always revealed in one's teaching and preaching. I cannot imagine a minister performing life-transforming ministry if he has hesitations about the inspiration of the Bible.

NEED-MEETING CHURCH

The backdoor phenomenon is a major concern of megachurches. A significant number of the people who come in through the front door of American churches leave through the back door. I believe that this is mainly due to inadequate pastoral care of the people. Many churches do not have an adequate pastoral care plan, which leads them to use untrained individuals to meet pastoral care needs. Although there are exceptions, most of these individuals are not able to meet the needs of the people. While all of us recognize that the pastoral care needs of even a small church cannot be fully met by the senior pastor, he or she must be responsible to ensure that the shepherding needs of the people are met by well trained individuals. Unfortunately, in many churches even the staff members closest to the senior pastor do not feel pastored by this individual. Their staff meetings may be more administrative than pastoral. Sometimes even care group organizational meetings are primarily administrative. The Church needs to understand the true meaning of 2 Corinthians 1:3-4: "Praise be to the God and Father of our Lord Jesus Christ, the Father of compassion and the God of all comfort, who comforts us in all our troubles, so that we can comfort those in any trouble with the comfort we ourselves have received from God." Care and comfort begin with God; we are to receive them for ourselves and then pass them on to others. This means that the senior pastor must truly care for his associates, and the associates ought to genuinely care for the care group leaders. Care group leaders need to pass on what they receive to the people under their care. Three or more levels of administration should be replaced with three or more levels of caring; there must be care beyond the hierarchy. Caring in this manner will close the back doors of many churches.

People come to church with diverse needs. Plans and programs should be in place to meet the multitude of needs represented among the members. Let us consider Abraham Maslow's hierarchy of human needs to examine my position. According to Maslow, the needs of human beings exist on different levels.[2] Physiological and survival needs constitute the lowest level. Above this level is the need for safety, which is followed by love and belongingness needs. Self-esteem needs follow belongingness needs, but the highest level of human need is the need for what Maslow calls self-actualization.

I agree with Maslow that human needs are distributed on various levels; however, due to the strong secular connotations of the term "self-actualization," I would like to consider the idea of Kingdom lifestyle. In my view, this occurs when an individual actualizes his or her fullest potential in God. In other words, when a believer fulfills God's purpose for his or her life, he or she is fulfilling a destiny. Kingdom lifestyle involves a life guided by the values of the Kingdom of God and lived in the power of the Holy Spirit. Kingdom values appear to be upside down, because they indicate that the first will be the last, dying is the way to live, and that giving is the method to receive. Nonetheless, the Kingdom of God is a kingdom of power because of the dynamic power of the Holy Spirit who is at work in the world today.

I present Maslow's model, not to defend a secular model, but to challenge the Church to address the totality of human needs. We often teach and preach as if the totality of human need exists at the lowest, or physiological, level of the hierarchy. Many churches have programs and forums to meet only some of the needs. Although para-church ministries can address selected needs, a Spirit-filled church would be remiss to address only one level of need. Few churches assess the total needs of the congregation and design ministries to meet those needs. Maslow's model is often visually presented in the form of a pyramid. He does not address spiritual needs, nor present a Christian perspective. I believe there should also be an inverted pyramid representing the various spiritual needs of people. Contemplating what this triangle would contain would constitute an interesting exercise.

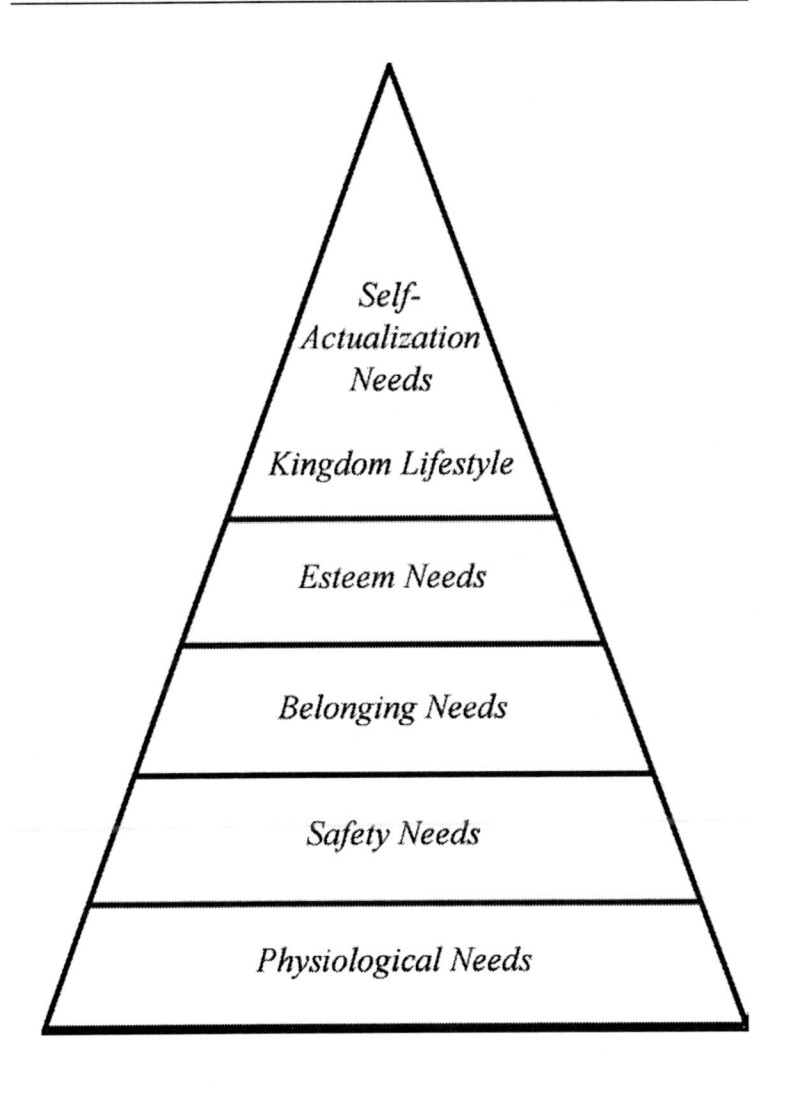

Self-Actualization Needs
Kingdom Lifestyle
Esteem Needs
Belonging Needs
Safety Needs
Physiological Needs

MASLOW'S HIERARCHY OF NEEDS

Preaching and teaching on the themes of basic needs, safety needs, belongingness, and self-esteem, along with Kingdom principles and Kingdom lifestyle, are desperately needed in our churches. Churches must intentionally design programs to address these needs. Only such churches will produce disciples of Jesus in this generation.

DISCIPLE-MAKING CHURCH
The development of seeker-friendly and user-friendly churches and services has become a matter of great importance in the church today. Although these are important matters, efforts to focus only on seeker-friendly services and not on methods to develop disciples will neglect the work for which we have been called. Christ's Church must be a disciple-making Church.

I like the model that Robert Coleman presents in *The Masterplan of Discipleship*.[3] He outlines how we can transform seekers into disciples, disciples into workers, and workers into leaders. His method is very biblical and practical. Unbelievably, some Charismatic churches do not have any form of Christian education or discipleship plans. A Spirit-filled church must be more than a place of celebration; it must be an incubator in which to mature disciples of Jesus.

The world today desperately needs disciples. The major business scandals of the new century revealed one thing very clearly. There is a great need for ethical people in our society. Chief executive officers of megacorporations were hauled off to the Capitol, or even to jail, because they disregarded ethics. Shocked by the situation, ethics courses are now mandatory in business schools across the nation. Business ethics is even being offered as a minor or major course of study. This remedial work should not be left to business schools; the church must do its part and make disciples. Society needs people who practice Christian ethics and Kingdom principles

I believe that the time has come to develop character-forming churches. Charismatic churches give much attention to the gifts of the Holy Spirit, but I believe that we must place equal emphasis on the fruits of the Spirit. The fruits of the Spirit are listed in Galatians 5:22-23: Love, joy, peace, patience, kindness, goodness, faithfulness, gentleness, and self-control. These are character qualities. God bestows the gifts, but the fruits need to be cultivated through time and work. The church ought to assist people in this cultivation through discipleship. No quick fixes apply in this area; only a disciple-making church can be a character-forming church.

A SPIRIT-FILLED CHURCH

The New Testament word for church is *ecclesia,* which means the assembly of those who are called. However, the word does not imply a building or a place of assembly. It involves people who are related to each other, not by being in one place, but by being connected to each other through the Head—Jesus Christ. The Bible calls the Church by several names, such as the bride of Christ, the body of Christ, family, the household of faith, and the temple of the Holy Spirit.

The Church is to be a different kind of community; it is to be a community of faith, transformed by the power of the Holy Spirit and not conforming to this world. Jesus' teaching on the Kingdom of God set the pattern that the Church is to follow. The Kingdom follows a different order from that of the world. As stated earlier, the first shall be last, the last shall be first, giving is the way to receive, and dying is the way to live in the Kingdom of God! The Church is called to be filled with the Spirit and led by the

Spirit, so that it may exemplify this new order through the grace of God and the power of the Holy Spirit.

Jesus Christ is the founder of the Church. His own words testify to this truth when He says, "I will build my Church." Therefore, any definition of the Church must conform to the Word of God. The Church is a congregation of the faithful who are called by God to join His family; they are called to be followers of Jesus of Nazareth, the Son of the living God. The Church must preach the Word of God, administer the ordinances, and facilitate the worship of God and fellowship of the saints. God calls the members of the Church. They are adopted into the family of God and set apart as priests for the purposes of God. Believers are to be led by the Holy Spirit to be a people of faith, hope, and love.

The Church has an organizational dimension, but it is truly a living organism. Any healthy living organism will grow and develop; in the same manner the Church must also grow and develop. God's Word and His Spirit sustain the life of the Church.

The Church has been saved in order to serve. God uses His apostles, prophets, evangelists, pastors, and teachers for the equipping of the saints to perform this work of service.

The Church is called to worship, evangelize, fellowship, and show mercy to the needy. According to Matthew, the last words of Jesus remind us that the mission of the Church is to go into ALL of the world, preach to ALL nations, and teach them to obey ALL things commanded by Him. Generally speaking, the Church is to continue the work of Jesus by engaging in preaching, teaching, and healing. God loves His Church and gives firm warning to those who would try to destroy it; He will not allow the gates of Hell to prevail against His Church.

The Church of Jesus Christ is a community of hope. We are "hope-bearers," and Christ in us is the hope of glory.

Our hope is not in some date or event; it is in the Person of the Lord Jesus Christ who lived, died, was buried, and rose again. He has ascended to heaven and is seated at the right hand of His Father. The hope of the Church is that He will come again to receive the Church. While no one knows the day or the hour of His coming, one thing is certain: "So shall we ever be with the Lord." The Church lives in this eschatological hope and shares that hope with the world in word and deed. The Church is a leaven of hope in this world. It is a reminder that God has a plan for His world and that His plan will be accomplished. The Church is also a herald, who invites people into the Kingdom of God and announces the coming of the King. The Church, by its very nature, is a sign to the entire world that God is in our midst and that He is at work.

AUTHORITY AND ACCOUNTABILITY

Pastors need administrative authority to conduct the operational affairs of their churches. A church's particular ecclesiology underlies the kind of authority its pastor exercises. I believe that one must avoid two extreme forms of exercising authority. The first involves a board or committee that keeps all administrative power to itself so that the pastor cannot implement the vision God has given him. In this type of church the pastor is simply a hired hand. Individuals on these boards are often control freaks who feel that God has called them to keep the preacher poor and humble. On the other hand, some pastors are dictators who are not accountable to any human person or group. Since pastors are human beings with normal human weaknesses, this is a risky situation for all parties concerned.

All ministers need accountability. The pastoral epistles list the required characteristics for people who are called to leadership positions in the Church. The book of Acts records that the apostles were accountable for their lifestyles and for their doctrines. Ministerial ethics also requires meaningful accountability. We invite deception by surrounding ourselves with individuals who are afraid of us and who may benefit from our indiscretions. What we actually need are spiritual fathers and elders who will grant us freedom, authority, and accountability. Many pastors have crashed and burned due to the lack of caring people in their lives who could speak the truth in love to them. This is an avoidable problem; instead of waiting for problems to develop, pastors and leaders of independent churches and ministries should initiate the establishment of an accountability system for their own protection.

PROSPERITY

There has been much misunderstanding in the Christian community regarding what is known as prosperity theology. Simply put, prosperity theology teaches that God wants to bless His children materially. It is unfortunate that this subject has caused so much controversy that some have decided to throw the baby out with the bathwater. It is true that some proponents of this theology have not used wisdom in their teaching, and others have used poor biblical exegesis to establish their doctrine. Yet human fallibility should not cause us to abandon the idea that God is good, and that He wants to bless His children in all areas of their lives.

I believe that context has a way of influencing one's theology. For instance, in India I have heard messages glorifying extreme poverty. Reflecting on that doctrine from a distance, I now realize that it had more to do with India's economy and Gandhian philosophy than with the Gospel of Jesus Christ. Likewise, in America I have heard extreme messages elevating earthly riches above eternal life. This may reflect the American economic context. I believe that biblical prosperity is different from both of these extremes. In my view, the material prosperity of Christians is a spiritual matter. While material prosperity or poverty is not necessarily evidence of one's spiritual maturity, God does bless His children in all areas of their lives. It is not difficult to establish that wherever the Gospel is accepted, the social status of the population rises. Some of the wealthiest and most highly educated people in India today are children of early Pentecostals, who were generally poor and uneducated people. In India, social indicators, such as literacy and women's health, are greatest where Christians live. Based on this evidence, I can easily believe that the Gospel elevates its followers. My own family has had such an experience.

The Bible speaks against the love of money, not against money itself. This issue seems to center around the difference between controlling and sharing; does the person control the money or is the opposite true? Does he give to those in need? I have met both rich and poor followers. Some, like Mother Teresa's Sisters of Charity, choose to be poor. Just as the Bible does not specifically explain the issue of the suffering of innocent people, scripture does not give simple explanations of material poverty. One thing is sure: Jesus came to announce good news to the poor. For these individuals, the message that they no longer have to be poor is truly good news. I do not believe that we should limit riches simply to the spiritual dimension of life. Spirit-led ministers should preach a *balanced* message of biblical prosperity, as they announce the good news to people of all levels of economic status.

A HEALTHY CONGREGATION

Modern Americans are growing increasingly concerned about their health. Although Americans spend billions of dollars on improving their health and well-being, in a context of the most advanced technology in the world national anxiety about health issues continues. The situation is similar in other developed nations. While people worry about their physical health, they often neglect their mental and spiritual health. Physicians say that many of our physical symptoms are rooted in psychological problems. Psychologists, on the other hand, say that the majority of our psychological problems can be traced to our unhealthy families and communities.

A healthy church is a healing community; it is a community of faith that fosters health and wholeness. But what does a healthy church look like?

Pastoral theologian Charles Gerkin recently described the five characteristics of a healthy Christian congergation. I believe that Pentecostal and Charismatic churches will benefit from examining themselves in light of Gerkin's categories. According to him, a healthy church is a (1) community of language, (2) a community of memory, (3) a community of inquiry, (4) a community of mutual care, and (5) a community of mission.[4] As we apply these principles to Pentecostal and Charismatic churches, we must aspire to be a *Spirit-filled* community of language, memory, inquiry, mutual care, and mission.

1. A Community of Language

The "language" that Gerkin refers to is not any particular native language, nor is it Pentecostal tongues; it has to do with the language, images, and metaphors contained in the Bible. According to Gerkin, we must become a community that uses biblical language, images, and metaphors. The Word of God should form and inform our worldview.

The power of biblical images to form a world view can be illustrated with the following example. The Bible contains the history of God's people in migration as well as exile. Migration and exile are two different things; while exiles are forced to live the way they do, migrants have a choice. However, according to these biblical images, we must see ourselves as aliens and pilgrims in this world, and we are to look for a city whose builder and maker is God.

2. A Community of Memory

A community of memory is one that remembers its past and focuses on the ways in which the Lord has brought it thus far. We are instructed not to forget all His benefits (Ps. 103:2). It offends God when His people forget His mercies.

Although the Lord has prospered the Pentecostals, there are a number of people who have forgotten how God brought them from the "wrong side of the track" to a place of honor. We must not forget our past and what the Lord has done for us. Moreover, we should teach our children about our spiritual heritage lest they forget their roots. This means that we must find ways to keep the memory of God's dealings with us alive. Instead of going after every wind of doctrine and every new voice, we must listen only to prophets and preachers who can teach us the truth and take us to a better future.

3. A Community of Inquiry

University students often tell me that the Charismatic community discourages them from pursuing education. This is especially true of mature theological students. Many think that only young people should be learners and ignore the fact that the whole world is moving toward the concept of lifelong learning. This is especially true in North America. All major corporations are supportive of employees' quests for lifelong learning. The world is changing so quickly, and new information is generated so rapidly that unless one remains a student for life, it is impossible to excel in one's field. The old "Sunday-School-is-for-kids" mentality must change in the Charismatic community. All must become students of the Word of God. Ignorance does not glorify God.

The opportunity to be a student must not be limited only to young adulthood; many user-friendly options for learning exist today. We must take advantage of these and not discourage adult learners. The average seminary student in North America is in his or her mid-thirties; these individuals have discovered that learning is the best form of investment.

Christians often fear that education will kill their desire for spiritual things. We must get beyond the fear of education; there are numerous living examples around us that learning does not have to kill one's enthusiasm for spiritual things. The journey toward becoming an inquiring community requires that the Church make a choice to search out and assess the profitable things of this world and the things of God.

4. A Community of Mutual Care

To ensure a good future for all of us, the Pentecostal community must find ways to care for one another. In order to become a truly caring community, we ought to seek the well-being of others in the Name of Christ. God has promised that as we seek His Kingdom, all the other things we need shall be added to us (Matt. 6:33). As we care for others, God's care will flow to us through multiple avenues. Ultimately, a healthy church is a caring community.

Although many churches are growing, not all of them are providing adequate spiritual support for their people.

Healthy churches train their members, formally and informally, to assist others who are struggling with various problems and needs.

5. A Community of Mission

American Charismatics need a missions strategy that is bigger than themselves. This may be true of churches outside the United States also. Charismatics have been too shortsighted in their strategy for world missions. Although short-term missions are a part of God's plan, we should not assume that God has exempted us from all long-term commitments. Charismatics can learn from Catholic and Southern Baptist missionary programs how long-term commitment of personnel and resources to particular geographical locations or people groups can make long-lasting positive changes. This is particularly true when local individuals are trained for continued leadership in ministry.

A healthy church is also concerned about the lost and dying. It is committed to reaching the world with the Gospel of Jesus Christ at any cost, because God so loved the world. The Gospel is global and must be shared with the whole world. God wants His Church to be a healthy one in memory, in words, in inquiry, in mutual care, and in missions. Blessed is the pastor who leads a healthy church!

Peter Wagner in his book, *Your Church Can Grow*, lists seven vital signs of a healthy church.[5] According to Wagner, a healthy church has a positive pastor who is full of faith and optimism. It also has a well-mobilized laity, and gives priority to meeting the needs of its members. A healthy church gives its members multiple opportunities for belonging; people need to be part of the gathering for celebration. They also need to belong to the congregation, the active community of faith, at that place. A small group, in which people can experience intimate belonging, is also important. This intimate dynamic will provide the accountability and growth opportunities that each believer needs.

Wagner also supports the controversial idea of homogeneous groups. He believes that having a particular social, economic, and racial majority is an important aspect of a healthy church. He also believes effective evangelistic methods and biblical priorities are important for the health of the church.

Ronald Sunderland, in his book *Pastor as Priest*, lists six elements of congregational growth and health.[6] According to Sunderland, a healthy church has a common identity and shares a common authority. A growing church shares a common memory, which includes the memory of the life, death, and resurrection of Jesus, as well as the local memory of the congregation. Christians must regularly tell the stories of the church, in order to keep the memories alive, so that even the newest members can become part of the story. Sunderland adds that a growing church has a common vision. A house divided against itself cannot prosper, but a common vision keeps the family of faith together. A growing congregation shares its life among its members, and it shares its life with the world.

The healthy church described in the book of Acts is a Spirit-filled church. As we have seen elsewhere, the Church in Acts is primarily a praying Church. Much of the book of Acts describes the apostles praying or going to prayer meetings (Acts 1:14; 4:31). The earnest prayer of the Church, on behalf of Peter in prison, is recorded in detail (Acts 12:5). A Spirit-filled church is a united church, as the Spirit moves where people are in unity (Acts 2:1). A Spirit-filled church is also a fellowshipping church (Acts 2:42) and a giving church (Acts 2:44-45). Since doctrines are important for every living church, a Spirit-empowered church should also be involved in study (Acts 2:42; 17:11).

The book of Acts demonstrates that a Spirit-filled church is a living organism; it grows and multiplies. The Church in Acts added and multiplied its membership regularly (Acts 2:41, 47; 6:1). The first Pentecostal church also emphasized praise and worship. A Spirit-led minister will lead the church to grow in all these qualities.

CHAPTER 5

COMPETENT CHARISMATIC MINISTRY

I will begin this chapter with a brief and simplified overview of the history of ministry. Christian ministry has its roots in the ministry of Jesus and His apostles, and Spirit-filled ministry, in its earliest stages, is described in the book of Acts. This is often called a period of apostolic ministry. This apostolic era was followed by the time of the Church fathers, whose ministry can be described as symbolic and sacramental. Subsequently, contemplation and seclusion prevailed, as Christian monks built monasteries through which to carry out their ministry. The work of pre-Reformation reformers and Reformers later called the Church back to its unsophisticated roots. During the Reformation, the emphasis of ministry was on the Word of God, while the focus of ministry was preaching.

The next stage of ministry included evangelical, missionary, and revivalistic ministry. Conversion was the primary focus of ministry during this period, particularly in America. The birth of the Holiness movement was the next stage of development, followed by the Pentecostal movement, at the dawn of the twentieth century. The Pentecostal movement emphasized tongues, healing, and holiness. The second half of the twentieth century witnessed the revolutionary development of the Charismatic movement. Charismatics emphasized prayer language as opposed to tongues as initial evidence, as well as miracles, signs, and wonders. The history of the church teaches us that as movements become institutionalized, new movements are born. One can only conclude that if the current Charismatic movement becomes institutionalized, another lively stream of God will appear. History illustrates that the Church made two mistakes throughout its history: The Church neglected its history and disallowed the free move of God's Spirit within its ministries. Both were costly mistakes.

The twenty-first century Church faces the challenge of determining the nature of Spirit-led ministry that is relevant to the new century. Such a ministry should reflect the lessons learned from history. Its model should be the ministry recorded in the New Testament, particularly in the book of Acts. It is my hope and prayer that a truly competent and Charismatic ministry will be the legacy of the twenty-first century Church.

COMPETENCE: A METHODIST MODEL

The Board of Higher Education and Ministry of the United Methodist Church compiled a list of functions, competencies, and characteristics of a pastoral minister. They identified fourteen functions, six knowledge competencies, and fifteen personal characteristics required of successful ministers. Charismatic ministers will benefit from studying these qualities. The following is the list of functions/duties of a pastoral minister who addresses the needs of the church and the wider community:
1. Preaching the Word— proclaiming God's Word.
2. Teaching— engaging the people in study.

3. Evangelizing— engaging the people to witness.
4. Leading in worship— administering the ordinances.
5. Engaging in connectional ministries— networking or denominational programs.
6. Supervising educational ministries— giving oversight to the total educational program of the church.
7. Counseling— premarital/marital, bereavement, and family counseling.
8. Visitation— visiting the homes of church members and the community.
9. Community ministries— participating in the life and work of the community.
10. Interdenominational ministries— participating in ecumenical services.
11. Recruiting future ministers.
12. Management of ministries such as goal setting, program planning, and evaluation.
13. Management ministries involving leadership development.
14. Administrative ministries such as budgeting, office management, record keeping, and personal accountability.

The knowledge competencies recommended by the Methodist Board are listed below:
1. Knowing the scripture.
2. Knowing theology or the doctrines of the church.
3. Knowing the history of the church.
4. Knowing church polity.
5. Knowing communication skills.
6. Knowing human relations skills.

Personal characteristics are listed below:

1. Self-awareness— knowing one's own gifts for personal ministry.
2. Openness to other people— willingness to relate to persons without regard to race, color, or social status.
3. Trustworthiness— regarding all pastoral conversations of a confessional nature as a trust between the person concerned and God.
4. Responsible self-control.
5. Openness to growth.
6. Loyalty and dependability.
7. Commitment to God.
8. Being an organized person.
9. Personal relationship with Jesus Christ.
10. Practicing spiritual disciplines.
11. Sensitivity to human needs.
12. Being a trustworthy person.
13. Willingness to be held accountable.
14. A passion for the sacredness of life.
15. Integration of vocation with personal and family well-being, and lifestyle.

Although these recommendations come from a denominational agency, they can assist nondenominational and independent Charismatic ministers.

STYLE OF MINISTRY

Craig Dykstra of Louisville Presbyterian Seminary, in a presentation on theological education, explained the concept of ministerial style. According to Dykstra, *style* can be defined as "fashioning of *power*"; it is the patterned manner in which one's energies are drawn together to have an effect on the surrounding world. *Power* here includes the combined effect of: (1) the minister's past experiences, (2) present situation, (3) thoughts, (4) feelings, (5) beliefs, (6) attitudes, and (7) values. Ministerial s*tyle* is expressed in (1) personal, (2) social, (3) cultural, and (4) spiritual dimensions of one's ministry. One's style of ministry is mostly unconscious.

Dykstra believes that ministerial *style* contains several underlying themes, which lie at a convictional level. We have convictions about: (1) ourselves, (2) our world, and (3) ultimate reality. Ministers ought to articulate their convictions, compare them with others' convictions, and with their own traditions, in order to develop a more excellent *style* of ministry. *Style* is changed only if convictions are changed. The examination of one's convictions requires the involvement of a trusted peer group. Many pastors address this need by entering the Doctor of Ministry program or other continuing education experiences.

BEING HEALTHY IN MINISTRY

Paul Pruyser's, *The Minister as Diagnostician,* has been helpful in my endeavor to define a healthy person.[1] In view of the fact that ministry is about making people whole, a minister of the Gospel must also walk in wholeness. Pruyser presents certain theological themes that are useful for ministers in their work of diagnosing the needs of people. I have found that these same themes reflect the characteristics of healthy persons.

One assumes that a healthy person is born again and baptized in the Holy Spirit. One should also assume that the individual maintains a wholesome Christian lifestyle or a sanctified life by faith. I believe that Pruyser's themes add to these characteristics of a healthy person. Pruyser's themes, with my definitions, are given below:

1) <u>Awareness of the holy</u>. A healthy person must be aware of the presence of a holy God in his or her life. People often describe their life issues in such a way that one wonders where God is in respect to their situation. An individual's awareness of the presence of God in his or her life is a sign of health.

2) <u>Sense of providence</u>. Providence is a theological term which means that God the Creator takes care of His creation. A healthy person is one who has an assurance that God will meet his needs, so that he can face the needs and issues of life from a position of confidence. God's providence covers His entire creation. A sense of providence enables an individual to live by faith, in the knowledge that God will supply all his needs through Christ Jesus (Phil. 4:19).

3) <u>Stance of faith</u>. Someone has said that faith sees the invisible, believes the incredible, and accomplishes the impossible. According to the writer of Hebrews, faith is the substance of things hoped for and the evidence of things not seen. A healthy person is one who looks at his world through the eyes of faith. Just as eyeglasses affect a person's vision, faith affects a person's view of life. A healthy person is one who walks by faith and not by sight alone. Faith enables an individual to believe in God's providence; faith believes that God is faithful. When we consider all the "by faith" statements in Hebrews chapter 11, it becomes clear that the

author is describing life as an adventure of faith. A healthy person must have that type of faith.

4) Experience of gratefulness. A healthy person lives a thankful life, in which his attitude is based on gratitude. Unfortunately, gratefulness is a rare commodity in an affluent society. A healthy person enjoys God's grace with gratitude. Gratitude does not depend on the size of the gift; it flows out of one's relationship with the giver.

5) Process of repenting. All born again Christians believe that God has forgiven their sins. The Christian life is a forgiven life. All of us, however, are subject to committing sins of commission and omission. This means that we must live with an attitude of repentance. The ability to experience *metanoia* (repentance), to ask for forgiveness, and to live in humility are evidences of a spiritually wholesome life.

6) Feeling of communion. Just as the Bible speaks about the communion of the saints, a sense of community fosters communion. A healthy Christian experiences communion with God and with the members of the community of faith. This extends beyond the sacrament of communion, to a sense of belonging and intimacy. A healthy person has the capacity for intimacy with God and man. All of us have met long-term members of a particular church who describe the church as "their" church. Regardless of the cause, this attitude reflects the absence of a sense of

communion with the body of Christ. Having a sense of belonging and community is a sign of health and wholeness.

7) <u>Sense of vocation</u>. Ministry is a vocation, which stems from a calling. In Christian life, all are called by God; therefore, all Christians must see their life's work, whatever that might be, as a vocation. Both plumber and preacher ought to live their Christian lives as vocations, but for the minister this attitude is an absolute necessity. A healthy person is one who sees his life's calling as a vocation.

Pruyser's themes, as I have defined above, are important clues to wholeness. Born again, Spirit-filled, and sanctified persons who demonstrate these qualities are truly healthy children of God. Ministers will benefit from examining their own lives with respect to these themes.

MINISTRY TO FAMILIES
American families are in desperate need of focused ministry today. The high rate of divorce and increased violence in homes and schools demand competent ministry to families. Often the church's ministry assumes that all members come from traditional nuclear families; however, statistics do not support this assumption. Worshipers and church members today represent all types of families. Many are from single parent homes, households headed by single women, or families in which children are parented by grandparents. Ministers require a special understanding of the needs of these men, women, and children.

Many cultural misunderstandings exist regarding marriage and family. The following is a partial list of such misconceptions:
1) Marriage is a contract, not a covenant.
2) Contracts have deadlines; they are not necessarily for life.
3) Marriage is a partnership, not a union.
4) The basic idea behind marriage is the concept of the significant other.
5) A spouse is a domestic partner.
6) In marriage, convenience is more important than conviction.
7) Family life and cohabitation are the same.
8) Childbearing and surrogate mothering are the same.
9) Material things are more important than the marital relationship.
10) Marriage should be tolerated, not celebrated.

Ministers must keep in mind that the only constant thing in family life is change. Just as individuals go through life stages, marriage also goes through predictable stages. Richard Dobbins, founder of Emerge Ministries, presents the following model of the stages of family:
1) Adjustment stage
2) Child-bearing stage
3) Child rearing stage
4) Child launching stage
5) Empty nest stage

Herbert Anderson in *The Family and Pastoral Care*, offers the following model of the stages of family development:
1) Forming the family (newlyweds)

2) Enlarging the family (children are born)
3) Expanding the family (children's world expands through friends)
4) Extending the family (in-laws are added)
5) Reforming the family[2] (original couple)

Essentially, both of these models present the same picture: Families are always changing. Ministry must address this constant change, as well as the people in each stage. Through reading and theological reflection, ministers can better understand the complex needs and issues of the people in these stages.

Ministers must also address the unhealthy state of many marriages in today's society. In his book, *A Marital Therapy Manual,* psychiatrist Peter A. Martin says that there are four types of sick marriages:

1) Deprived marriages where one feels deprived by the other partner.
2) Marriages in which one of the partners, particularly the husband, is in search of a mother.
3) The double parasite marriage, where both partners are exploiting each other.
4) The paranoid marriage, where the couple is fearful of everyone else and believes that people are actually working against them.

Martin lists the qualities of healthy marriage partners as follows:

1) Capacity for independence and interdependence
2) Capacity to support one's mate
3) Capacity to accept support
4) Capacity to have physical intimacy
5) Capacity to have emotional intimacy[3]

Ministry must address the need for healing in sick and broken marriages. Ministers can meet the various needs through preaching, teaching, and counseling as well as through church programs and para-church organizations. Although no perfect families exist, we must encourage families to be as functional and wholesome as possible. The church, as the household of faith, must also be wholesome and functional. Experts have identified several symptoms of dysfunctional families. According to one source, dysfunctional families have three rules by which they live: (1) don't feel; (2) don't trust; (3) don't talk. In these families, members are not allowed to have feelings; feelings are neither owned, nor freely expressed. Family members do not trust each other, and the family lacks open communication. In order to avoid speaking unpleasant things, issues are not verbalized. This fosters unhealthy secrets within the family, which eventually undermines the entire family.

According to Herbert Anderson, wholesome families have three healthy areas: (1) roles, (2) rules, and (3) rituals.[4] In a healthy family, each member has a definable role to play, and each functions normally in that role. In crisis, however, members are able to exchange roles in a healthy way. Dysfunctional families, on the other hand, have confused roles. Members do not know how to exchange roles based on the current situation. Healthy families also have explicit rules by which they live. Each party in the family knows the rules, but the rules are negotiable. Parents do not wait to explain the rules until their children have broken them. Members can also question outdated rules and renegotiate more appropriate rules. Dysfunctional families live by rigid rules; they maintain outdated rules and are threatened by any attempts to negotiate them. Family rituals represent healthy habits, because they are predictable and dependable. For example, the family expects that a birthday will be celebrated. Worship is also part of the normal family schedule. Rituals provide security, because everyone in the family knows what to expect.

Unfortunately, some churches are also dysfunctional. Lessons for a healthy family can also be applied to parsonages and churches. Ministers must remember that the most effective ministry occurs when the church provides a healthy model to follow.

MINISTRY TO WOMEN

Ministry to women requires a special understanding of their needs. Pastors should recognize that women face many disadvantages in our society, particularly if they are part of an ethnic minority. Studies show that, on average, a woman pays a higher price for a car than a man, if she goes alone to make the purchase. Products geared specifically toward women often carry a higher price tag. Women are charged a higher price for everything from shampoo to automobiles.

Our culture sends many conflicting messages to women, and the church often inadvertently reinforces these cultural messages. For instance, Christie Neuger lists the following paradoxical messages:
1. You are valuable as a woman because of your nurturing and relational capacities; but as a culture we value independence and autonomy.
2. You must be submissive, patient, and supportive in your family life; yet why have you not left your abusive husband—you must, at some level, like the violence.

3. Your true vocation is to be domestic and nurturing, but culture rewards and pays those whose work is outside the home.
4. An intimate male partner must protect you; yet one third of all female homicides are committed by husbands or "lovers."
5. You can be anything you want to be; however, sixty percent of all females in the work force hold clerical and retail positions, or service jobs, in which at least 75 percent of their colleagues are female.[5]

Women in ministry also report that they face many issues in the church. More liberal women testify that they are oppressed through male dominated theology, worship, history, polity, leadership, and seminary classrooms. According to Duane Parker of the Association of Clinical Pastoral Education, female clergy are looking for the following:

    1) A new form of worship
    2) A sense of community
    3) Recognition of their contributions
    4) A sense of collegiality
    5) Equal employment and pay
    6) Non-hierarchical polity
    7) Ordination regardless of gender[6]

Women's ministry was not a major issue for the early Pentecostals; unfortunately, this cannot be said of today's classical Pentecostals. Happily, women's ministry is much less of a problem for independent Charismatics; the ministries of Joyce Meyers, Lindsay Roberts, and others prove this fact. Women in Pentecostal groups find it difficult to attain ordination, especially if they have any desire to pastor. Most ordained candidates are para-church ministers or foreign missionaries. Some scholars believe that the issues among Pentecostals related to the inspiration of scripture and the ordination of women are problems contracted from Pentecostal association with evangelicals. One can only conclude that there was a price to pay for the respectability they obtained by joining the National Association of Evangelicals!

According to Kay Marshal Storm, persons ministering to women in today's culture should be prepared to deal with issues related to the following problems:
1) alcohol and drug abuse
2) child abuse
3) molestation as a child or of a child
4) incest
5) infidelity
6) rape
7) suicide
8) teen pregnancy and unwanted pregnancy
9) wife abuse
10) issues of suffering[7]

Storm gives males the following advice for ministering to women:
1) Don't be physically involved.
2) Don't encourage dependence.
3) Don't force the male perspective.
4) Don't ignore one's own prejudices.

Jesus considered ministry to women very important. He ministered to women and allowed women to minister. Even the Apostle Paul, whose words feminists often quote to attack the church, endorsed and praised the ministry of women. The Church of Jesus Christ must continue its ministry, part of which is to empower women to minister to others. Ministry in the twenty-first century must include ministry to women and ministry by women. One task of the global Church is to discover culturally appropriate ways of involving women in ministry, and to engage in the process of transforming culture.

MINISTRY TO CHILDREN

Children's ministry is a special need in today's church. Senior pastors cannot leave this ministry to another department of the church; all ministers, especially senior pastors, should have a deep understanding of the needs and issues of children today. The fact is that children are neglected in our churches, often due to the unmentionable reason that they are not financial contributors. Children are frequently idealized, and viewed as being free from problems. Many times, childcare is seen as women's work. In reality, pastors lack training in ministry to children, and their feelings of inadequacy keep them away from this ministry. We must remember that the church is the family of God and the household of faith. A family is a place in which every child is valued and cared for. The house of God must not be an exception to this rule.

From a theological perspective, children are significant. The mystery of the incarnation is a sign that children are important to God, since God became a child. The infinite became an infant! Christ exhorts us to be childlike, and challenges us to have childlike faith. "Let the little children come to me, and do not hinder them, for the kingdom of God belongs to such as these" (Mark 10:14).

According to Andrew Lester children need their ministers to offer the following:
    1) A sense of competence
    2) Positive attitudes and values

3) Confirmation or correction of their perceptions
4) A sense of belonging
5) A friend and a hero to look up to
6) Listening ears
7) Acceptance of their feelings
8) Spiritual guidance [8]

Lester believes many methods are available to minister to children, such as play, art, and storytelling.

The Gospels illustrate that Jesus was concerned about children, and that He was comfortable with them. He healed and blessed children, even to the point of aggravating the disciples. The Church must continue this tradition of ministry that values little children. The Catholic Church faced serious charges against their priests, regarding their treatment of children, at the beginning of the twenty-first century. However, neglect or abuse of children is not just a Catholic problem, it is a Christian problem. Modern society contains enough threats against children; even schools have become dangerous places. All servants of God must participate in the nurturing of children, so that the house of God can be a safe haven and a place of healing for all the children of the world.

INSTITUTIONAL MINISTRY

While Pentecostals and Charismatics are experts in church planting and church growth, until recently they neglected the potential of institutional ministry. Institutional ministries include military chaplaincy, health-care chaplaincies, industrial chaplaincies, and other forms of ministry not directly related to the local church. It appears that American Pentecostals appreciate the need for long-term foreign missions, whereas Charismatics specialize in short-term missions. However, both groups have a difficult time seeing the tremendous needs and ministry opportunities that exist in the major institutions of this country. Traditionally, these institutional ministries have been dominated by mainline denominations. The mainline denominations have organizational structures in place to supervise the training of candidates and "endorse" them for these ministries. Pentecostal denominations, such as the Assemblies of God and Church of God, saw the potential for these ministries first, but Charismatics are also beginning to see the need. Colonel Jim Ammerman was a pioneer in promoting Charismatic ministry in the Armed Forces. He started the Chaplaincy of the Full Gospel Churches organization and has been very active in recruiting and assisting seminarians with their military chaplaincy placements.

Institutional ministry requires special professional preparation. I will present only a brief description of that process here. Education and training are the first requirements. Most professional ministry positions in institutional settings require a Master of Divinity degree, which is a three-year post-baccalaureate degree. Normally, the degree must be earned at a seminary that is professionally accredited by the Association of Theological Schools in the United States and Canada (ATS). Additionally, a candidate must receive ordination by a recognized faith community. It can be a local church, denomination, or network of churches. Most chaplaincy positions in hospitals, prisons, and the military require an additional endorsement from the proper authority of the particular faith community. Denominations have their boards and commissions to do this work. Independent Charismatics can work with organizations such as the Chaplaincy of Full Gospel Churches (Rev. E. H. "Jim"

Ammerman, President and Director, 2715 Whitewood Drive, Dallas, TX 75233-2713).

Clinical training beyond the Master of Divinity is required for many professional positions. The best training is called Clinical Pastoral Education (CPE). The Association for Clinical Pastoral Education (ACPE) offers training for seminary students and graduates across the United States. This organization has a rich history and offers training at Basic, Advanced, and Supervisory levels in hospitals, clinics, and other centers. The training includes practical experience, classroom work, group processing, and personal supervision by a certified supervisor. Most seminaries offer academic credit toward the Master of Divinity degree for CPE training.

CPE training is offered in units or quarters. Generally speaking, one unit involves 400 hours of training offered in three months, but some centers offer part-time extended units. CPE is a challenging experience for most candidates, as it challenges the trainees personally and professionally. Tuition is required for the training; however, most centers providing one-year programs offer a stipend to cover the cost and at least some of the living expenses. Normally, year-long programs are offered to individuals who have at least one basic unit completed. The ACPE headquarters in Decatur, Georgia can supply additional information on its training programs and centers.

Association for Clinical Pastoral Education
1549 Clairmont Road, Suite 103
Decatur, GA 30033-4611
Telephone: 404 320 1472

The Canadian Association of Pastoral Practice and Education (CAPPE) is the Canadian counterpart of ACPE. They can be reached at the following address:

CAPPE
47 Queen's Park Crescent East
Toronto, ON M5S 2C3
Phone: 416 977 3700

Professional certification is also an important part of preparation for institutional ministry. The most prominent professional organization is the Association of Professional Chaplains (APC), formerly the College of Chaplains. A seminary degree and CPE training qualify candidates to become members of the APC. Members who have four units of CPE and one year of experience in chaplaincy can apply for certification as Board Certified Chaplains (BCC). The address of APC is given below.

Association of Professional Chaplains
1701 East Woodfield Road, Suite 311
Schaumburg, IL 60173
Telephone: 847 240 1014

Official credentials alone do not guarantee effective, Spirit-filled, institutional ministry. Credentials may open the door to a ministry position, but personal competence will prosper an individual in that position. Good chaplains must possess interpersonal and intrapersonal competences. Intrapersonal skills require a strong sense of personal identity; this includes an awareness of one's own strengths and weaknesses as a person and minister. A chaplain should also have an awareness of his own dynamics, as well as an understanding of his needs for personal growth. An effective institutional minister should be an integrated person, as personal wholeness is an important ingredient of success in institutional ministry. This type of minister can also affirm himself. When ministry exists outside the walls of the church, no immediate community of faith is available to offer affirmation. The minister who is unable to affirm himself in a wholesome way will find the work very difficult.

In the area of interpersonal relationships, an institutional minister needs the skills to work in a multireligious community, without losing his convictions or spiritual gifts. Individuals who are able to effectively communicate within their professional contexts do well in this ministry. A Spirit-filled minister, working in a multicultural context, must possess much wisdom in today's world. Christian ministry is not value neutral; an individual should not give up his values to work in a non-Christian environment. On the other hand, he will encounter much resistance and hostility if he employs only confrontational strategies. Recall that many saints worked in Caesar's palace during St. Paul's time. One can work with others and still minister effectively, as the Lord opens the door for such ministry.

An effective institutional minister must be able to initiate, maintain, and appropriately terminate relationships with others. The minister should effectively utilize personal and ministerial authority in his relationships. An increasing number of Charismatic ministers are entering institutional service. Most of them are successful in their ministries; however, some who cannot make the contextual adjustment find it difficult to stay in this work. Institutional ministry is in need of more workers. I would like to encourage everyone who has a sense of calling to this ministry to pursue the required professional preparation.

PRAISE AND WORSHIP MINISTRY

I must say a word about the music ministry in Pentecostal/Charismatic churches, and the involvement of young people in this ministry. As a member of the North American immigrant community, I am very pleased to see the involvement of young people in the life of the church. I have often argued with church leaders in favor of including and involving young people in the various ministries of their churches. Although some quarters initially resisted, most bilingual churches are now open to involving young people in certain aspects of their worship and ministries.

Providing leadership for praise and worship seems to be the area in which young people are most frequently involved. Many young people are gifted in music, and a good number of them are skilled at playing a musical instrument. I am glad to see the Lord using them in the ministry of music. New life has emerged in many churches through the influence of young people, who bring more contemporary tunes into the services. I am concerned, however, over certain tendencies that have emerged in the youth music ministry. I believe the following fifteen suggestions would help praise and worship leaders improve the effectiveness of their ministry.

1. **Check Your Calling.** It is wise to confirm that you are called to the ministry of leading praise and worship. Do you have talent? Do people seem to sense God's presence when you lead them in worship? Do you consider your talents a gift from God, and do you desire to use them to glorify God and bless people? Enter into this ministry only after you have confirmed these issues within yourself. Don't assume you are called to music ministry just because someone else is doing it, or because you can play an instrument.

2. **Check Your Life.** If you are not living a sanctified life by the grace of God, it is better to voluntarily get off the stage. Worship led by an individual involved in unconfessed sin does not please God. Your testimony and credibility are a major part of your ministry. Before you approach the pulpit to minister to others, repent of your sins and be reconciled, as far as possible, with all people.

3. **Choose Songs Prayerfully.** Not all good songs are suitable for all occasions; the selected song must be appropriate for the ministerial occasion. Consider your purpose. Do you wish to lead people to praise God? Are you giving people an opportunity to dedicate themselves to God at the end of a service? Choose songs that are appropriate for the occasion and fitting to the specific portion of the service.

4. **Be Under Authority.** Do not take over the service in order to lead where you want to go. Always inquire about the goals of the service from the person who is in charge and identify how you can help reach those goals. Learn the order of service and discover its theme, so your music ministry will reinforce the major theme of the service.

5. **Watch Your Appearance and Body Movements.** Leading praise and worship is a ministry, not a performance; dress modestly and decently. While the rhythm of music influences the movement of one's physical body, a Christian minister's physical movements should not imitate worldly performers. Your movements and appearance should not distract people from worship. As much as possible, be culturally appropriate to the congregation; do

not present yourself as a worldly person. Avoid all appearance of evil.

6. **Draw Attention to Jesus, Not Self.** Do not yield to the temptation to show off your talent in a way that draws attention to yourself rather than to God. Give your best, but don't cause people to focus their attention on your gifts and talents; keep your ego in check. Lead people to the throne of God, and let them see Jesus. You must decrease and Jesus must increase. People know talent when they see it, and they will appreciate you when they know you consider your talent a gift from God. This does not translate into putting yourself down. Humility is not denying the gift God has given you; rather, it is giving God the glory for the gift you have. Do not promote yourself over God.

7. **Promote the Word.** Some worship leaders drown the words of songs in loud music. Keep in mind that we worship with hymns, psalms, and spiritual songs; the words are important. Let the music serve the Word, not the other way around. Since faith comes by hearing and hearing by the Word of God, allow the Word to prevail.

8. **Minimize Your Own Words.** Some music ministers talk too much between songs. If your calling is to preach, seek training and enter into a preaching ministry; do not camouflage yourself as a praise and worship leader and hold up the worship services. Lead the congregation to sing and glorify God with few words, and focus on leading worship.

9. **Respect Time.** Find out before the service how much time has been set aside for praise and worship and stay

as close to the guideline as possible. When God is doing something in the midst of His people, it can be difficult to stop. Seek permission to continue at such times. Most service leaders will be sensitive to this; however, do not go against the presiding person and take over the service.

10. **Acknowledge Your Team.** Do not try to be a superstar and take all the glory if your team does well. God uses each musician differently, so acknowledge the contribution of your team members. Ministry is not a one man show.

11. **Listen to the Message and the Altar Call Carefully.** The concluding songs should flow with the message that was preached. If there was an altar call, the music should support it. The songs should also respect the mood of the service. Change or add to pre-planned songs appropriately, if your team can handle it, and make smooth transitions.

12. **Motivate, Rather than Manipulate.** Music is a powerful vehicle, which can be used to motivate as well as manipulate. Be led by the Spirit and do not try to manipulate people. You cannot create a revival. Flow with the Spirit and allow the Lord to move by getting out of His way.

13. **Avoid Tampering with the Loudspeaker.** Prepare the speaker system for your needs before the service begins, as much as possible. Tampering with the sound system and instruments for a lengthy period of time, in the middle of a service, is very distracting to the worshipers.

14. **Let God's People Sit.** If a lengthy song service is planned, please allow the congregation to be seated during part of that time. At least give permission to those who wish to sit down, so that they will not feel that they are dishonoring you and God by being seated. Most services have older or handicapped persons who are unable to stand up for a lengthy period of time. Remember that people stand up by themselves when God moves.

15. **Remember Uzzah.** Second Samuel 6 tells of a man named Uzzah, who touched the Ark of the Covenant. Though his intentions were good he died because he was forbidden by the Law to touch the Ark. This happened while David, the great psalmist, led worship. Ministry may seem like something anyone can do. In some circles, the person with the loudest voice and most aggressive personality is the "minister." This is not the biblical pattern. Ministry is a calling, and it must be performed humbly. Even in the New Testament, the sacred is guarded and we are called to holiness and humility. Paul says that "unworthiness" causes many to "sleep" or to die; therefore, we must handle ministry with joyful fear and grateful humility. Leading praise and worship is a great ministry, which should not be taken lightly. Lead with skill and enthusiasm, as well as with humility and joy. Then watch heaven open.

CONTINUING EDUCATION OF MINISTERS
(This section is an update of an article published in *The Clergy Journal* (Vol. LXXI, Number 1, October 1994).

Well-meaning individuals often exhort ministry candidates using the words of the Apostle Paul, "Study to shew thyself approved . . ." (2 Tim. 2:15, KJV). Unfortunately, the exhorters seem to forget that these words were written to someone who was already in ministry. The apostle's words have more to do with the continuing development of a minister than with his or her pre-ordination studies.

The church in America has always been concerned about the training of clergy. Historically, however, the attention of theological educators has been focused on the formal education of ministry candidates. Today the emphasis is shifting to ministerial continuing education.

History

According to Robert T. Frerichs, the modern movement of continuing education for ministry can trace its roots to the late nineteenth and early twentieth centuries.[9] For instance, historical evidence indicates that clergy gathered together on the frontier for the purpose of studying biblical exposition, polemics, practical theology, and elocution.

The Chautauqua movement, which began as a Sunday school movement and later became an adult education movement, had a tremendous impact on continuing the education of clergy in the early part of this century. Later, the land-grant universities played a vital role in the development of clerical continuing education. Eventually theological seminaries and denominations began to provide seminars, schools, and refresher courses.

The 1930s witnessed the founding of many clinical pastoral training programs. In the fifties and sixties, several organizations were born that influenced the continuing education of protestant ministers. Among these were The Interpreter's House at Lake Junaluska, founded by Carlyle Marney; the Pastoral Institute of Washington; the Institute of Advanced Pastoral Studies, founded by Reuel Howe at

Bloomfield Hills in Michigan; the Society for the Advancement of Continuing Education in Ministry (SACEM); and the Academy of Parish Clergy.

The most notable development in the 1970s and 1980s was the development and explosive growth of Doctor of Ministry degree programs. Studies have shown that status enhancement and aspirations for upward mobility are not the primary or decisive motives of most D.Min. students; rather, they are motivated by their continuing education needs.

Needs

Careful studies of the continuing education needs of ministers have been conducted among clergy of different cities, regions, and denominations. According to James Berkley, ministers generally need remedial, retooling, and renewing education.[10] Connolly C. Gamble, Jr. identifies needs according to the following categories: knowledge, growth, skills training, support systems, and therapy.[11]

Charles B. Fortier reports the following facts resulting from a study he conducted: (1) practically all of the clergy assessed expressed a great need for continuing education in relation to their various professional roles; (2) the practical areas of administration, public relations, and communication skills seemed to be of great interest; (3) clergy need to increase their competence in relation to counseling, race relations, drug problems, adolescent development, administration, and Christian education.[12]

Donald Emler studied the continuing education needs of clergy in relation to their mid-career development.[13] He looked specifically at United Methodist ministers, focusing on the continuing education needs of clergy based on their functional roles. The following educational needs were identified by mid-career ministers: improvement in communication skills; educational ministry skills; counseling skills; basic administration skills, such as multiple staff relations; and organizational development skills, such as planned change strategies. The study also identified understanding current trends in theological development as a need for ministers who had finished seminary training at least fifteen years earlier.

Jimmy Ward Walker prioritized the following continuing education needs of clergy, based on a study of the relationship between pastoral tenure and continuing education among Southern Baptist ministers: counseling, leadership, organizational development, church growth, evangelism, personal spiritual development, theological issues, personal development, social issues, preaching/communication, teaching, relational skills, and personal ministry.[14] Although the relationship between pastoral tenure and continuing education was insignificant, his study showed that a pastor's formal education was a major determining factor of his commitment to lifelong learning.

Other studies have identified the following additional needs for ministers: skill in group dynamics, theological development, combined lay-clergy educational experiences, self-acceptance, social action skills, conflict resolution skills, and enabling of others.

In a national survey of interdenominational chaplains which I conducted in 1992, I identified forty learning needs in three major areas: (1) professional skills, (2) knowledge, and (3) personal development. The highest rated needs in the professional skills area were: counseling, conflict resolution, and spiritual direction. The three top knowledge needs were: ethical issues, current theological issues, and spiritual development. The following were at the top of personal development needs: spiritual renewal, financial management, retirement planning, and self-care.[15]

Why Continuing Education?

Professionals are responding in different ways to today's changing society and the ongoing information explosion. A common response involves development and implementation of continuing education programs for practitioners. Ministry cannot afford to ignore this issue. Most clergy are practicing their profession in a world that is much different from that in which they were trained. They are forced to gain additional knowledge and skills to minister more effectively to persons traveling on the information superhighway. It is high time for all churches and denominations to require and fund ministerial lifelong education.

Unfortunately, it appears that ministers are tempted to take a fast food approach to continuing education rather than a planned meal approach. Ministers would be better off assessing their own learning needs and intentionally planning to meet those needs. Fortunately, many learning resources are available today to meet the felt needs of the clergy.

Resources

The Doctor of Ministry degree program is a major resource for ministers with professional qualifications; it is now available in about ninety seminaries. A great number of clergy are not able or willing to pursue a doctoral degree to meet their continuing education needs, despite the popularity of the D.Min. program. Fortunately, seminaries and Bible colleges do offer several types of non-degree continuing education programs.

Clinical Pastoral Education (CPE) is a widely used resource for the continuing education of clergy. CPE involves a structured educational process designed to increase pastoral effectiveness in counseling, pastoral care, and mental health ministries. Today, CPE training is available in hospitals, parishes, campuses, and correctional and geriatric facilities, as well as in seminaries.

The Society for the Advancement of Continuing Education in Ministry (SACEM) is another major resource for clergy of all denominations. SACEM offers information on continuing education opportunities available in various formats, in the following areas: biblical studies, spirituality, worship and preaching, theological and ethical issues, leadership and administration, human relations, religious education, social and justice issues, career development, ecumenical and interfaith studies, missions, and evangelism.

Self-initiated projects present another avenue of learning for clergy. These not only include personal use of books, journals, magazines, and audio or video tapes, but also meetings with colleagues for the purpose of learning from each other. According to one published report, thirteen ministers from Louisville, Kentucky met periodically to help each other become better preachers. Their "preaching seminar" was self-initiated and cost effective. It began when one concerned minister reached out to his colleagues in the area.

Private and public universities continue to be great resources for ministers. Courses in counseling, communication, administration, and religious studies are available at these institutions.

Professional associations for clergy are proven resources of continuing education. The Academy of Parish Clergy, the Association of Professional Chaplains (formerly the College of Chaplains), the American Association of Pastoral Counselors, and the Association of Mental Health Clergy, constitute examples of associations that offer continuing education opportunities for ministers. Pastors' schools and leadership conferences sponsored by independent ministries, as well as various denominations, are also resources for ministers.

Undergraduate and graduate degree programs are now available for clergy through external seminary programs, Bible colleges, and universities. In addition to the traditional correspondence courses, various innovative delivery systems are now available. Charles Snow, an adult educator, lists the following systems: extension courses where instructors are transported to the external sites, establishment of extension centers with some permanent faculty, packaging courses in short-term modules so the student is on campus only for short periods of time, and construction of independent directed-study courses. Non-degree programs are also available through the non-traditional avenues.

High technology has also opened up new continuing education resources for clergy. For example, telephone and internet conferences are very common in many states. Several audio/visual educational conferences are simultaneously aimed at social workers, clergy, and other professionals. These explosive developments in high tech, communication, and the internet have created more innovative means of lifelong education for the clergy.

Oral Roberts University School of Theology and Missions and the ORU School of Healing and Ministry, offer many academic and non-academic programs, respectively, for Pentecostal/Charismatic ministries. Information about these programs is available on the internet at www.oru.edu.

USEFUL WEB SITES

Society for the Advancement of Continuing Education in Ministry (SACEM)
www.sacem.com

Academy of Parish Clergy (APC) www.apclergy.org

CHAPTER 6

PREACHING IN THE POWER OF THE SPIRIT

God made the decision to save the world through the "foolishness" of preaching. All Christians have been touched by this foolishness at some point in their life; somewhere, someone preached Jesus to us, and that is what brought us to this new way of life. Biblical preaching is still converting the world and confounding the wise.

I believe there is a difference between the foolishness of preaching and foolish preaching. A lot of preaching today, much of it by untrained preachers, is simply foolish. We have our share of lazy preachers who refuse to study and deliver the Word of God to the people of God in the power of the Holy Spirit. Extemporaneous, superficial preaching hurts the body of Christ. Many ministers seem to have time for everything but study. As the dean of a seminary, this is a matter of great concern to me. At Oral Roberts University, we do all that we can to offer workable programs and schedules to busy pastors, in order to help them with their studies. Oral Roberts University School of Theology and Missions offers modular and distance education programs to degree-seeking and non-degree seeking pastors. ORU offers everything from unaccredited ministry institute courses to a Doctor of Ministry program, approved by the Association of Theological Schools in the United States and Canada (ATS). Much effort and planning go into these programs because of our commitment to improve the quality of ministry in the Pentecostal/ Charismatic world.

I tell potential theological students that there is a difference between butchers and neurosurgeons, even though both groups use knives. The butcher produces dead meat, whereas the surgeon produces healing and wholeness. Many ministries can only be characterized as butcher ministries because sincere persons, with good intentions but no preparation, sensed the call of God and went out to minister. Although they lack biblical knowledge and ministerial skills, many of them believe their ministry is adequate just because they are able to draw a crowd. Unfortunately, many of their sheep are wounded and must escape through the back door to seek healing from other ministers and counselors. God's Word is a double-edged sword and in untrained hands it can be a dangerous weapon. Faith is the substance of things hoped for and the evidence of things not seen, but toxic faith is a killer.

We all recognize that schools do not make ministers; it is God who calls persons to ministry. But called persons must subject themselves to training in ministry. Billy Graham said that if he had his ministry to do all over again, he would make two changes: first, he would study three times as much as he had. "I have preached too much and studied too little," said Graham. Secondly, he would give more time to prayer.

In a letter Graham wrote to John R. W. Stott, he quoted Donald Grey Barnhouse, a well-known Philadelphia pastor: "If I had only three years to serve the Lord, I would spend two of them studying and preparing."[1] It took the disciples of Jesus three years of training to do ministry in the primitive world of two thousand years ago. It seems unlikely that less training could produce a competent minister for this complex information age.

I am grateful for the many pastors and leaders who come to the seminary to continue their education and training. They spend time with the faculty and other ministers in a process that can only be characterized as iron sharpening iron. They examine their theologies and ministry practices and improve their skills. As a result, these individuals can implement their newly acquired ministerial skills in their churches. I have visited the churches of many ORU graduates where, according to church members, the ministry has improved from passable to exceptional, or from excellent to beyond excellent.

The New Testament strongly testifies to the importance of preaching, as a chief component of Christian ministry. Notice the following passages:

> What then shall we say, brothers? When you come together, everyone has a hymn, or a word of instruction, a revelation, a tongue or an interpretation. All of these must be done for the strengthening of the church (1 Cor. 14:26).

> Speak to one another with psalms, hymns and spiritual songs. Sing and make music in your heart to the Lord, always giving thanks to God the Father for everything, in the name of our Lord Jesus Christ (Eph. 5:19, 20).

> Let the word of Christ dwell in you richly as you teach and admonish one another with all

wisdom, and as you sing psalms, hymns and spiritual songs with gratitude in your hearts to God (Col. 3:16).

Preach the Word; be prepared in season and out of season; correct, rebuke and encourage— with great patience and careful instruction (2 Tim. 4:2).

Teaching is also an important function of ministry, which often operates in conjunction with preaching. The Apostle Paul modeled this ministry very well: "So for a whole year Barnabas and Saul met with the church and taught great numbers of people" (Acts 11:26). The order of worship in the synagogues of the first century provides insight into the priority of preaching in the early church, as synagogues served as meeting places for early Christians. As Christian believers left the synagogues for other places of worship, they took with them many aspects of Jewish worship. According to William Hendriksen, the following is the typical order of synagogue worship:

1. Thanksgiving or blessing given before and after the *Shema*: "Hear, O Israel, the Lord our God, the Lord is one, and you shall love the Lord your God with all your heart, and with all your soul, and with all your might."
2. Prayer with response of "Amen."
3. Reading of a passage from the Pentateuch with translation into Aramaic.
4. Reading from the prophets with translation.
5. Sermon or word of exhortation.
6. Benediction by a priest or a closing prayer when the priest was not present.[2]

The words of Luke 4:16-21, as well as early Church history, confirm this outline. William Willimon outlines early Christian worship in his book, *Pastor: The Theology and Practice of Ordained Ministry*, which shows the similarity between early synagogue worship and Christian worship.[3]

CHRISTIAN WORSHIP
(FIRST APOLOGY OF JUSTIN MARTYR, A.D. 90)

(1) On the day which is called Sunday, all who live in the cities or in the countryside gather together in one place. (2) The memoirs of the apostles or the writings of the prophets are read as long as there is time. (3) Then, when the reader has finished, the president, in a discourse, admonishes and invites the people to practice these examples of virtue. (4) Then we all stand up together and offer prayers. (5) And, as we mentioned before, when we have finished the prayer, bread is presented, and wine with water; (6) the president likewise offers up prayers and thanksgivings according to his ability, and the people assent by saying, Amen. (7) The elements which have been "eucharistized" are distributed and received by each one; and they are sent to the absent by the deacons. Those who are prosperous, if they wish, contribute what each one deems appropriate; and the collection is deposited with the president; and he takes care of the orphans and widows, and those who are needy because of sickness or other cause, and the captives, and the strangers who sojourn

amongst us in brief; he is the curate of all who are in need.

A public service described in Nehemiah 8:8 gives the outline of preaching in the Old Testament: "They read from the Book of the Law of God, making it clear and giving the meaning so that the people could understand what was being read." It appears that reading, translation, and explanation were involved in this exercise. Other scholars, such as Aldwin Ragoonath, believe that Old Testament preaching had three parts: reading, translation, and explanation with application[4]. The purpose of preaching was to make the Law clear to the people; increasing their understanding for the purpose of obedience was the deeper goal. New Testament preaching must pursue the same purpose, even though the Law has been replaced with a new law of grace.

Several types of preaching exist. According to Ralph G. Turnbull, preaching can be categorized into twenty-five different types, including topical, situational, psychological, dispensational, missionary, ethnic, and others.[5] The most commonly used sermons can be categorized as topical, textual, or expository.

Historically, the prophetic preaching of the Old Testament was the first type of preaching identified. Modern textual/expository preaching evolved in the synagogue movement, which began during the captivity of Israel. It is clear that Jesus approved of such preaching. He attended synagogue worship, not only in Jerusalem, but also at other locations (Luke 4:16-21, Matt. 9:35, Mark 1:21). According to Luke, synagogue attendance was His custom (Luke 4:16).

Ragoonath provides a very helpful study of the New Testament words for preaching and teaching to support the idea that biblical preaching is the ideal. I will simply present the list of words and their meanings here.

KERUSSEIN = declaration, announce good news

EUANGELIZESTHAI = to proclaim good news, to declare Gospel of salvation

MARTUREIN = witness (testifying personal experience)

DIDASKEIN = to teach, to deliver didactic discourse

PROPHETEUEIN = Prophet

PARAKALEIN = exhorting

Gerhard Friedrich's definition of a prophet is relevant in this regard: "The prophet is the Spirit-endowed counselor of the community who tells us what to do in a specific situation; who blames and praises, whose preaching contains admonition and comfort, the call for repentance and promise."[6] The Apostle Paul describes a prophet as an individual who offers exhortation, edification, and comfort (1 Cor. 14:3). As such, Paul's description supports the idea of prophetic preaching in the New Testament.

According to Ragoonath, a good sermon possesses the following qualities:
1. It is biblical. A good sermon must be based on the Word of God.
2. It applies clearly to people's situations and needs. Effective preaching addresses the needs of the listeners.

3. It results from reflective thinking. Superficial preaching does not impact congregations. Reflective thinking provides deeper insights.
4. It is pastoral. Sermons must reveal a shepherd's heart.
5. It is positive. Even unpleasant issues can be dealt with in a positive manner.
6. It is delivered naturally. A good preacher is true to his own personality and natural attributes such as voice, gestures, etc.

EIGHT PREACHING PRINCIPLES

Ragoonath also posits the following eight crucial principles for sound preaching:

1. Highest view of Scripture - The preacher must perceive the Bible as the inspired Word of God.

2. Adequate preparation - The preacher must do his homework.

3. Textual/expository - The sermon must be biblical.

4. Homiletical Order - The sermon needs logical order that should be derived from the text.

5. Relevant - The message must be relevant to the situation and need of the listener.

6. Christocentric - Jesus Christ must be the center of the message.

7. Evangelistic - The message must share the good news.

8. Pastoral in nature - The message should be given from a shepherd's heart.[7]

Gijsbert D. J. Dingemans maintains that preaching should have three levels.

1. A level of explanation, information, and clarification for teaching.
2. A level of proclamation, persuasion, and appeal to transmit the power of the text to move and confront.
3. A level of basic trust and interrelationship, in order to show the credibility of the text, church, and preacher for consolidation and confirmation of common faith.[8]

Pentecostal preachers must take into account the tremendous challenge that all Christian preachers in the twenty-first century face: Modern America embraces religious pluralism, which basically believes that all gods are equal. The best of Christianity has always shown respect for other religions, but present society demands acceptance and endorsement over and above respect. One cannot endorse all religions as viable spiritual paths and simultaneously declare the uniqueness of Jesus Christ. The task of overcoming societal challenges in order to preach the Gospel will be an ongoing challenge for all evangelicals in North America, but particularly for Pentecostals and Charismatics who are committed to the Full Gospel perspective.

Charles Snow, professor of preaching and leadership at Oral Roberts University School of Theology and Missions, recently outlined some of the challenges faced by biblical preachers in our day. He believes that biblical communicators must find creative ways to share the life-giving message of the Gospel with today's digital generation. Bill

Easum's assessment of the current culture is relevant. Easum makes the following observations:

North America is now one of the prime mission fields in the world.
1. Many forms of truth are replacing ultimate truth.
2. The twentieth century emphasis on property and the importance of place is being replaced by an emphasis on relationship and community.
3. The Digital Age has already replaced the Information Age.
4. People are moving to the cities, and boats are no longer coming from Europe. The new immigrants are coming from Hispanic and Asian cultures.
5. Bio-genetics is beginning to rearrange our understanding of human actions to the extent that we will soon be able to attribute anything to "my genes made me do it."[9]

Rick Warren adds:
1. Proclaimers of truth do not get much attention in a society that devalues truth.
2. The majority of Americans reject the idea of absolute truth.
3. They value tolerance more than truth.
4. Moral relativism is at the root of what is wrong in our society.[10]

Regardless of popular opinion, we must continue to preach the Gospel and declare what we believe. Christianity has often preached to a hostile world. Somehow the foolishness of preaching works because the totality of preaching is more than what the preacher says and does.

In any case, preachers must avoid the three handicaps listed by Tim Timmons:

1. The world is looking for quick-fix answers.
2. The Church has gotten used to talking to itself.
3. The sermon and worship experiences are directed at those who own the church.[11]

Trevor Grizzle, professor of New Testament at Oral Roberts University Seminary, recently presented a preaching seminar. He defines New Testament preaching as evangelistic in intent, as it unfolds and applies the implications of the Gospel to lead the believer into greater discipleship and maturity in Christ. Grizzle stated, "New Testament preaching is more evangelistic, more democratized (Acts 8:4), Christ-centered, and is attended often by the miraculous." According to Grizzle, the Old Testament prophets were forerunners of New Testament heralds. Their messages were always "practical, pointed and vivid."

Grizzle describes the preacher as God's ambassador (2 Cor. 5:20; Eph. 6:20), a medium of God's power, and a megaphone of God's voice (Acts 2:14). A preacher has a sense of oughtness and urgency (Mark 1:38; Acts 4:20; 1 Cor. 9:16), and he is a transparent person who adapts his presentation to his audience (Acts 14, 17, 22). According to Grizzle, the content of New Testament preaching includes the following:
1. The good news about the Kingdom of God and the Name of Jesus (Acts 8:12).
2. The death, resurrection, and exaltation of Jesus (Acts 2:23-24).
3. The Lordship of Jesus (Acts 2:36).
4. A summons to repent and receive forgiveness (Acts 2:38; 3:19; 5:31; 10:43).
5. Christ's return (Acts 3:21).

Grizzle lists nine essentials of New Testament preaching:
1. Christ-centered
2. Spirit-empowered
3. Simple and practical
4. Contemporized biblical saving acts of God
5. Adapted to the audience
6. Attended by the miraculous
7. Demands response and offers hope
8. Bold confidence in call, calling, and message
9. Targeted and purposeful

Biblical preaching is, by nature, goal-oriented; we preach for a response. Lawrence Lacour, former professor of preaching at Oral Roberts University, asked his students: "Why preach if you don't expect a response? Why preach if there is no call to response?" He compared preaching to selling cars. "Why do you go through the whole sales process if you have no plans to make people sign on the dotted line at the end?" he asked. We must keep in mind that there are at least three reasons for preaching: to give information, to convince or persuade, and to motivate action.

Biblical preaching has homiletical order; the text supplies the logic of the message. According to Ragoonath, one can discover it by finding the Holy Spirit's intent in the text. "The preacher must be a logician and a rhetorician," said Luther.[12] This does not mean, however, that preaching is just a commentary on the text. Martyn Lloyd-Jones said, "Preaching is not a running commentary. It has form, pattern and relevance."[13] The most important aspect of preaching is what God speaks to the people through the message.

Dennis F. Kinlaw in *Preaching in the Spirit,* makes several constructive suggestions for modern preachers. He advises preachers to read well, emphasizing that the Bible should be our primary, but not exclusive, reading. Kinlaw recalls Oswald Chambers' words: "A man who reads only the Bible never really reads the Bible."[14] Good preaching can offend the hearers from time to time. One should not hesitate to preach on issues of the day as needed. John Wycliffe, for instance, preached against popes, confession to priests, and materialism in the church. The preacher must remember that when it comes to evangelistic preaching, he or she is never the first witness in the hearer's life. The Holy Spirit is at work preparing the way long before the preacher arrives.

Good preaching is not just a matter of technique; the relationship of the preacher to the people is also a very important factor. The preparation of the preacher as a vessel of God is the most important aspect of Spirit-filled preaching. We offer that which we have received. Kinlaw says that the preacher plays the role of a midwife; God reached us through Jesus Christ, and Christ reaches the world through us.

Pentecostal preaching is not just an explanation; it is an event. Something happens as the Word of God is preached. It takes place at the intersection of the preacher, the people, and the Word of God, and it happens through the intervention of the Holy Spirit. Pentecostal preaching is preaching in the power of the Holy Spirit. Recently I received a videotaped sermon that Oral Roberts, chancellor of Oral Roberts University, delivered at a church in Chicago just a few weeks ago. I was impressed with the power of his preaching at the age of eighty-four. I know that I witnessed more than just his physical stamina; in fact, he was sitting down during the delivery. But the power of the Spirit was strongly evident in his preaching. Pentecostal preaching is that kind of powerful preaching.

Esteemed scholar David Buttrick lends powerful support to the previous statement, when he says that preaching is phenomenological. He describes preaching as an event, which forms faith consciousness in the individual and the community. Preaching is more than an explanation of the text or a discourse on psychological well-being; preaching forms a faith world in which we may live and love. Buttrick says that revelation is not something that is just written or reported; it is something that happens. Revelation is not just out there or back in history, and preaching should not be reduced to an explanation of past events to a current congregation. Preaching must participate in God's ongoing redemptive purposes. From my perspective, this implies that preaching should leave open the possibility for biblical revelation to happen again. To a certain extent, Buttrick seems to describe the preaching of the Gospel with signs following, which is what Pentecostal/Charismatic preaching should be.

What is unique about Pentecostal preaching? It is the preaching of the Gospel, anointed by the Holy Spirit. It is preaching about Jesus in the power of the Holy Spirit. Pentecostal preaching involves the body, mind, spirit, and emotions of the preacher in the declaration of the Word of God under the inspiration of the Holy Spirit. Simply put, Pentecostal preaching is preaching by a person filled with the Holy Spirit.

A SAMPLE PENTECOSTAL SERMON

The following is a sermon I delivered at a Pentecostal convention in Florida in 2003.

The Kingdom and the King

Text: Matt. 13:45 & 46 (NIV)
Again, the kingdom of heaven is like a merchant looking for fine pearls. When he found one of great value, he went away and sold everything he had and bought it.

Acts 2:36 (NIV)
Therefore let all Israel be assured of this: God has made this Jesus, whom you crucified, both Lord and Christ.

Jesus came preaching the Kingdom of God; His message was the Kingdom. He preached the Kingdom of God to people outside the Kingdom and taught the principles of the Kingdom to his disciples. His entire life and ministry manifested the power of the Kingdom of God. Our message should also be the Kingdom of God.

According to the Word of God, the Kingdom of God has arrived; His kingdom arrived when Jesus came into the world, for He said, "The Kingdom of God is at hand." The Kingdom of God has three dimensions; first, the Kingdom has come. Second, the Kingdom of God is here now; it is in your midst, manifesting the power of the Holy Spirit. Third, the Kingdom of God is coming. The cosmic fullness of the Kingdom of God is yet to come. What is the Kingdom of God? According to the Apostle Paul, the Kingdom of God is not meat or drink; it is righteousness, peace, and joy in the Holy Spirit!

Preaching the Kingdom of God is not a safe occupation. John the Baptist came preaching the Kingdom of God, and he was beheaded. Jesus picked up the message saying, "Repent for the Kingdom of God is at hand," and He was crucified. His disciples continued the message and they also had to pay with their lives.

God always finds individuals who will declare the arrival of His Kingdom, and that declaration begins with a call to repentance. The world does not like such a call, but Kingdom life begins with repentance. In the Gospels, "repent" is not a request; it is a command. Jesus told Zacchaeus, "Come down!" and to Matthew He said, "Follow me." To the rich young ruler Jesus said, "Sell." These are not meant as requests; they are commands.

We are all familiar with the idea of naturalization, the process through which an immigrant becomes a U.S. citizen. Unfortunately, no one is naturalized into the Kingdom of God; one must be "born again." Two kingdoms exist— the Kingdom of darkness and the Kingdom of light— and you must die in one to enter the other. More specifically, you must die in one to be born into the other. The Kingdom of God is a kingdom of light and a kingdom of life. As we enter the Kingdom of Life we pass from death unto life.

Kingdom life is unique. In the Kingdom, formation is more important than information. The Kingdom is governed by the principles of agape love. This love goes beyond neighborly love or brotherly love and becomes trinity love. What does trinity love look like? According to Juan Carlos Ortiz, author of the well-known book, *Disciple*, it looks like mashed potatoes.[15] You can claim unity just by being together with others, like potatoes in a sack. They can sit in the bag and sing about unity, saying, "We are in the same bag, and we have the same brand name." They could also say, "I am a big potato and you are a small potato;" or, "Look at me, I'm a white potato, you are a brown potato." Often, this is the only kind of unity that we have in the Church. But if you take the potatoes out of the bag, peel them, cut them into pieces, put them in a pot, and boil them to make mashed potatoes, something happens to these potatoes. They are the same potatoes, but now no one can distinguish the big potato from the small potato. One cannot tell the difference between the white potato and the brown potato because they have become one. This kind of love represents trinity love, which allows us to sing, "We are one in the Spirit; we are one in the Lord." The authentic Kingdom life is a life of love and unity.

Most of us are not used to agape love, because it is unconditional love. We have become accustomed to conditional love, which I call "if" or "because of" love. God presents us with "in spite of" love, and He desires that we be filled with this love. Several years ago, I met a woman in Tulsa who told me that she had learned how to prevent cancer. She gave me her secret: drink as much carrot juice as you can, three times a day. She has been practicing this strategy for many years, and I believe it works. She is healthy, and she has no cancer, but she has one slight problem: She now looks like a carrot! If you fill yourself with carrot juice long enough you will begin to look like a carrot; similarly, if you fill yourself with the love of God long enough, you will begin to look like the love of God. When people see you approaching, they will no longer say, "Here comes trouble," or "Here comes gossip;" instead they will say, "Here comes the love of God." Brothers and Sisters, be filled with the love of God.

The Kingdom of God is filled with Godly relationships. Kingdom relationships are like the human body; all are members of one body, uniting each other, supporting each other, passing along nourishment to each other, and making room for each other. In the Kingdom we are not in competition with each other, and we don't attack each other. Recently, psychologists were studying stress and its impact on people. They used rats and inflicted stress on them in order to observe the effects. First, they ran the rats through a maze. Next, they placed some cheese at the end of the maze, and continued to run the rats through. After the rats got used to receiving a food reward, the psychologists removed the food and ran the rats through again. The first time they were confused at the end of the maze, wondering why there was no food. They went back and ran again, only to find that there was still no food at the end of the maze. The stress level of the rats began to increase, and they eventually began to bite each other. Christians should not act like rats. Only the devil benefits when believers fight among themselves. Unfortunately, we are often guilty of enriching the enemy by fighting among ourselves. God is calling us to Kingdom Life; may we manifest the lifestyle of the Kingdom of God in all that we do.

In the Kingdom, the King is preached. A lot of Christian preaching is Old Testament preaching. Although we should not neglect the preaching of the Old Testament, we must preach it as New Testament people. We are instructed to preach Jesus Christ and Him crucified. The disciples preached and healed the sick in Jesus' name, even though they were questioned and specifically told not to preach in Jesus' name. They were also beaten for preaching in the Name of Jesus. The book of Acts describes how Philip the evangelist explained the book of Isaiah to the eunuch. Although Philip began in the Old Testament, with Isaiah, the Bible tells us that he preached Jesus unto him. Amazingly, the eunuch requested to be baptized in water. Scripture does not recount that Philip told him about baptism; yet apparently preaching about Jesus includes teaching about baptism. One can begin preaching in Isaiah and conclude with baptism in Jesus' name.

The first Full Gospel sermon is recorded in the book of Acts, chapter 2. Only five verses of that chapter mention the Holy Spirit, even though the entire book of Acts is based on the acts of the Holy Spirit. Only seven verses in the first sermon involve the Holy Spirit, but seventeen verses relate to Jesus! Jesus is more than a Savior, and He is more than a healer; the Jesus of the Gospel is Lord. The theme of the first sermon was Jesus and His lordship, and three thousand people responded to that message. Jesus must be the center of the Gospel. Just as the earth is not the center of the solar system, the Church must not become the center of the Gospel. The Gospel is the Gospel of Jesus Christ, and Jesus is Lord of all. The Church is filled with members who have accepted Jesus as Savior and Healer, but to whom Jesus has not become Lord. Jesus must become the Lord of our lives; His lordship is the primary foundation of the Kingdom of God.

Christians need a new revelation of who Jesus is, just as Peter needed such a revelation. Jesus asked His disciples, "Who do men say that I am?" and they recounted the various perceptions of the public. Then Jesus made the question more personal, asking, "Who do *you* say that I am?" Peter responded, saying, "Thou art the Christ, the Son of the living God." Jesus replied that it was not flesh and blood that had revealed this truth to Peter; in other words, Peter was receiving a revelation. A true understanding of Jesus' identity cannot be gained through academics and reading, even when the book we study is the Bible. It is something that the Father reveals to us through His Spirit.

Thomas the disciple also had a revelation of Jesus. Thomas was not present at the time that Jesus appeared to his disciples after the resurrection. When the other disciples reported their experience, Thomas found it hard to believe. Later, Jesus appeared to Thomas and invited Thomas to examine His wounds. Thomas did not investigate the wounds of the Master; instead he cried out, "My Lord and my God!" Thomas experienced a revelation of the lordship of Jesus. In those days, only the Roman emperor could be called "*kurios*," or lord; thus, the Romans would have been greatly angered by Thomas' confession. Similarly, the Jews would have taken offense to Thomas calling Jesus "*theos*," or God. But Thomas could not contain his confession; he had a revelation and was compelled to exclaim, "My Lord and my God".

As the creeds of the Church testify, the Church fathers knew who Jesus was. For example, the Nicene Creed describes the "Father" using twenty-one words and the "Spirit" using thirty-four words. In contrast, one hundred and thirty-three words are devoted to Jesus. The Church fathers knew the importance of Jesus as the revelation of God to man. Jesus Christ is King of Kings and the Lord of Lords. This confession is not scientific; it is a matter of faith. Science deals with natural, visible, and measurable matters, but the Bible pertains to visible and invisible things. Mankind is not saved by information; we are saved by faith. It is by faith that we know Jesus Christ is the Son of God, and it is by faith that we are convinced in this matter. By means of faith, God has given us the grace to know who He is. This knowledge includes various truths. By faith, we believe in His virgin birth, and we believe in His miracles. We also believe in His death on the cross, in His resurrection, and in His ascension. It is by faith that we also believe in His soon return.

Yes, the Word became flesh and dwelt among us. His Name is called Emmanuel, "God with us," signifying that Jehovah the eternal one has become flesh and dwelt among us. *Elohim*, the Great God of glory, *Elelion*, the Most High

God, and *Elshadai*, the all-sufficient God became flesh and dwelt among us. *Adonai*, the Lord and Master God, became flesh and dwelt among us. God, in Christ, reconciled the world unto Himself, and all the fullness of the Godhead was in Him. Jehovah *Jirah* our Provider God, Jehovah *Rapha* our Healer, Jehovah *Nissi* our Banner, and Jehovah *Shalom* our Peace, became flesh and dwelt among us.

God became man in Jesus. Jesus went about performing good works, as He fed the hungry, healed the sick, and raised the dead. After three years of ministry, He was crucified. Amazingly, the infinite became an infant for us; the Creator became creation for us. He is greater than sickness, greater than the devil, and greater than death; He is greater than the grave. Jesus is Alpha and Omega, the Beginning and the End, and Jesus Christ is King of Kings and Lord of Lords. The Kingdom of God belongs to those who make Jesus Christ the King of their lives; may He be more than a Savior or Healer to you. Jesus said that if two or three are gathered in His name, He is there in the midst of them. By faith, look to Him and cry out, "My Lord and My God," and make a commitment to follow Him as a disciple and a citizen of the Kingdom of God.

CHAPTER 7

TEACHING AS JESUS TAUGHT

Jesus was a master teacher. Professor Howard Ervin reminds his students that Jesus preached the Kingdom of God, manifested the power of the Kingdom in His public ministry, and taught the mysteries of the Kingdom to His disciples. Often the disciples asked Jesus privately for detailed explanations of the parables and issues He discussed in public. He revealed truth to them and explained mysteries to them that He did not reveal to the public, in order to help them gain insights. The Gospels describe many moments of discovery among Jesus' disciples.

Teaching is a very important ministry. Today's Church is in desperate need of well-trained teachers and Christian educators. The current generation's tendency to make short-term commitments has affected the church in the area of Christian education. It is unfortunate that some Charismatic churches do not have any intentional Christian education programs; in some circles the entire ministry of the church has boiled down to celebration!

Jesus called His disciples to preach, TEACH, and heal. The teaching ministry of the Church must not be neglected.

A church that does not teach is short-sighted, and it will have no future. We are called to make disciples of all nations, in order to teach them to obey everything Jesus has commanded (Matt. 28:20). This cannot be done without adequate planning, preparation, and commitment of resources.

Christians are commanded to "grow in the grace and knowledge of our Lord" (2 Pet. 3:18). Without a learning process one cannot grow; yet it is unclear who is responsible to provide this opportunity. Christian education should not be left to untrained, volunteers; neither should it be the sole domain of church ladies. I believe that the senior pastor of a church is responsible to ensure that adequate teaching and training opportunities exist in the church. A healthy church is a learning community, and all members of this community, including the pastors, must be learners. Christian life involves lifelong learning.

Churches of the new century are in need of a Bible-based, Holy Spirit-empowered teaching-learning process, which should involve all members of the faith community. When each member learns how to apprehend and obey God's purpose for his life in Jesus Christ, he will be able to serve effectively, at his level of functioning, in some form of ministry. The ultimate purpose of such a program should be to make mature disciples who will be imitators of the Master Teacher, Jesus, in this generation.

JESUS, TEACHING, AND THE HOLY SPIRIT

Jesus must become the model teacher in the pulpit, as well as in the classroom. Several writers have identified Jesus' qualities as a teacher. Jesus, as a teacher, was a man of love, excitement, and optimism. He was an approachable teacher who believed in an informal way of teaching. Jesus taught as one with authority, yet profound simplicity. Jesus emphasized the pupil, not Himself, and He always started with the student's needs. Jesus was not a boring teacher because He believed in using a variety of teaching methods, such as questions, discussions, lectures, and stories. He often incorporated everyday objects as teaching aids.

A good teacher must make room for the Holy Spirit to move in his classroom, as the Spirit is the principal teacher who will lead us to all truth. This ultimate truth is Jesus, who described Himself as the Way, the Truth, and the Life. The Holy Spirit helps both the teacher and the students, and He prepares the environment for the proper transmission of truth. First, the Holy Spirit enables the teacher to understand the truth; then He opens the mind of the student to receive the truth. Without the assistance of the Holy Spirit, the impact of teaching is limited.

The purpose of teaching is not just the simple transfer of information; Christian education is transformational. Studying God's Word involves change and transformation. Instead of conforming to the world, God calls us to be transformed by the renewing of our minds. This transformational process should be the basic transaction of teaching.

EDUCATIONAL PHILOSOPHY

Christian educators need a philosophy of education. Philosophy deals with reality, truth, and value. In the realm of reality, educators must deal with the nature of the learner and the role of the teacher; the area of truth must be addressed by the curriculum; and the area of value addresses ethics, helping us understand what is good and valuable. In Christian education the learner can be defined as one loved by God; he or she is someone for whom Jesus died on the cross. The role of the teacher is to teach and to embody the life that he teaches; modeling is the best form of teaching.

The teaching curriculum is the Word of God; it is Truth with a capital "T." For a Christian educator, the Truth of

God's Word is not negotiable; it is not truth with a small "t." This is a difficult concept for twenty-first century people to fathom, because this generation takes pride in its faith in relativism. We are so used to updating scientific truths that we have a difficult time believing in a Truth that is established forever. To define what is good, we look to God and to His Word; His plans for our lives are good. A good Christian educator is mindful of this. Before Oral Roberts University was founded, its founder and current chancellor, Oral Roberts, shook the world with the simple statement "God is a good God." He received much abuse for stating that basic truth from Psalm 118:1, because the culture could not handle it at that time. Oral Roberts University as a Christian educational enterprise was built on the idea that God is a good God, and that He wants to bless His creation!

A Christian educator should not approach people of other faiths with contempt. Stanley Jones, the great missionary statesman who devoted his life to teaching the Hindus of India about Christ, taught us this lesson. Christians do not need to profane the names of other gods in order to share their faith in Jesus Christ. Releasing the floodlight called Jesus does not translate into cursing the darkness around us; we accept people as they are, and we love them where they are. Then, like Paul at Athens, we can introduce the Truth of the Gospel in a way that people can understand. Our goal is not to colonize the world; rather, it is to share the love of God that is shed abroad in our hearts. As Christians we must seek to release the light we received from Jesus into the dark corners of our world. We want to share the life we have discovered in Him with our world, for we live, move, and have our being in Him.

GOOD TEACHING

Teaching must rely on more than the brain of the student in order to be effective. According to Larry Richards, good teaching must involve understanding, emotions, values, and decisions on the part of the teacher.[1] It takes patience, presence, and persistence to be a good teacher of God's Word. Patience allows a teacher to lovingly accept the student, and presence represents availability without invasion; persistence means presenting God's truth faithfully. Thus, teaching is more than just talking or letting the students talk. It must extend beyond the classroom or the sanctuary and incorporate planning, inspiring, caring, and modeling.

Teachers should also consider their students' ability to retain information, as illustrated by the following:

Percentage of Information Retained	**Of what they**:
10%	Hear
30%	See
50%	See and Hear
70%	See, Hear and Say
90%	See, Hear, Say and Do[2]

If this is the case, pastors and teachers need to do more than talk. Leonard Sweet, in *Postmodern Pilgrims,* states that students in the postmodern world are: (1) experiential, (2) participative, (3) image-based and (4) connected (on line).[3] This means that teachers need to incorporate new methods to enhance learning, such as video, PowerPoint, drama, storytelling, and dialogue, as opposed to monologue, debate, and group exercises. Stated more technically, learning involves three domains within the student: the affective, the cognitive, and the behavioral (psycho-motor).

The *affective* realm primarily involves feelings and emotions; in this area a teacher should aim to create inspiration in the student. The *cognitive* domain involves students' knowledge and intellect. Students will grow in this area to the degree that the teaching content is effective. The *behavioral* area of learning impacts the will and the activities of the student, and will be reflected in his or her lifestyle.

The twenty-first century has ushered in a culture of entertainment, reverse values, violence, and materialism. Christians are called to communicate the Gospel to such a culture. In order to meet this challenge, we need to do more than just pursue business as usual. Pastors must acquire an adequate understanding of how people of all ages learn and then apply that understanding to their teaching ministry. Competent teachers are needed to teach children and adults.

ADULT EDUCATION

The last part of the twentieth century witnessed the growth of the field known as adult education. Malcolm S. Knowles is considered the father of the adult education movement. Known as *andragogy* (learning of adults), as opposed to *pedagogy* (learning of children), this field studies adult learners.[4] Although it can be said that good pedagogy techniques would also be effective as andragogy, there are some unique aspects of adult education that do not fully apply to children. For instance, Knowles suggests that there are five assumptions of adult education that should be taken seriously by teachers of adults.

About	Assumptions Pedagogy	Andragogy
Concept of the learner	Dependent	Self-directing
Role of learner's experience	Not sufficient as a resource	Rich resource for learning
Readiness to learn	Uniform by age, etc.	Develops from life tasks
Orientation to learning	Subject-centered	Problem-centered
Motivation	By external rewards or punishment	Internal incentives or curiosity[5]

By considering Knowles' perspective, pastors will be able to avoid teaching adults as if they were children. A teacher is more than an individual who provides information; he or she must become a guide and mentor to the students.

The sole purpose of some teachers is to enable students to commit information to rote memory. A teacher who instructs and tests based on this goal, only measures the student's ability to memorize. Although it is a good thing to memorize the Word of God, according to Benjamin Bloom, memorization is the lowest level of cognitive activity. Bloom lists six levels of intellectual learning, ranging from the lowest to the highest:
1. Knowledge: Student is able to recall.
2. Comprehension: Student is able to explain the information.

3. Application: Student can use the information in a meaningful way.
4. Analysis: Student can see the relationship between concepts.
5. Synthesis: Student is able to combine ideas and see the bigger picture.
6. Evaluation: The student is able to make informed judgment.[6]

According to Raymond Wlodkowski, an effective teacher of adults is a good facilitator, who exhibits the following four characteristics. First, he or she will have *expertise* in the field of teaching. For example, a Bible teacher must have a good knowledge of the Word of God. Secondly, a good facilitator has *empathy* toward the student. Empathy helps the teacher present the material with a special concern for the learner's needs. A good facilitator is *enthusiastic* about the student, the subject, and the teaching-learning process. Finally, according to Wlodkowski, a good facilitator possesses *clarity* of thought and presentation.[7]

An effective facilitator also models what he or she teaches, and acts as an expert resource person who knows the subject area well. He or she must be a good counselor who is interested in the learner's academic, as well as non-academic life, and can act as a guide for the learning process using a variety of teaching methods.

Ultimately, a good teacher wants to move the adult student from a dependent learner to a self-directed learner. This requires the teacher to frequently change his role from coach to salesman, to facilitator, and to consultant. The Foundation for Critical Thinking presents the following tactics for promoting active learning:
1. Have the student summarize what has been taught in his or her own words.

2. Elaborate on what has been said.
3. Relate the issue being discussed to the student's own life experience.
4. Give examples to clarify and support what is said.
5. Show connection between related concepts.
6. Let the student state the question at issue.
7. Let the student restate instructions in his or her own words.
8. Describe to what extent his or her current point of view is similar or different from the teacher's or others.
9. Put a response into written form.
10. Write down the most pressing question on the student's mind.
11. Discuss any of the above with a partner.

It appears that adults learn best when teachers use methods which:
1. Reduce anxiety.
2. Let the student show what he or she knows.
3. Give clear directions.
4. Show the relevance of the lesson.
5. Value the accuracy of responses or activities over the speed of response.
6. Repeat the information and allow deep processing.
7. Pace the lesson presentation at a reasonable speed.
8. Avoid distractions and interference.
9. Give both visual and auditory stimuli.
10. Make sure that the student is physically comfortable in the classroom.[8]

The teaching ministry of the Church has not matched the challenge of the postmodern world. Postmodern society imposes so many major issues on individuals that they clearly require more resources than the ability to quote a verse or two. Individuals must be taught to make decisions and abide by them as Kingdom citizens in this world. In this way believers can develop the capacity to make internal decisions about their lifestyles.

TEACHING TEENS

I recently conducted a training seminar for Pentecostal Sunday School teachers of teens in New York City. Teachers and leaders from more than thirty-five immigrant churches in the New York area gathered in one place for this teachers' training event. Sponsored by the regional leaders of an association called Sunday Schools of North American Keralites, the sessions were attended by men and women from all walks of life who teach adolescents in churches.

After conversing with pastors and teachers at this seminar, I became convinced that teacher training, particularly for those teaching teens, is a tremendous need in our community. Often the teachers we recruit for these classes are untrained volunteers or people who do not feel a calling to teach teens. This is a grave mistake. Christian education is serious work that is to be conducted with concern and competence.

Christian education is also an issue of international importance. Teacher training must become an important matter for the Church in all continents. The world's modern information generation requires specially trained teachers. I attended Sunday School before the age of overhead projectors and multimedia computers. Today's teens do not live in that old world, and the instruction they receive in their secular schools is much different from what I experienced. I am not sure that they will respond significantly to a "business as usual" type of Sunday School.

Consider the fact that teenagers today are the first generation that has access to information without supervision.

Previously, we went to teachers as authority figures and experts for information. Teachers still need to present information, but much information is available to the students even before they meet the teacher. Modern teaching must take this reality into account.

Most of us grew up with a teaching method that conceptualized teaching as pouring information from the teacher, the big bucket, into the pupil, the little bucket. This pedagogical model is now outdated. Teachers need to provide more than information; students must also be taught what to do with the information, in order to apply it properly. They should also develop the capability to evaluate the information for truthfulness and faithfulness to the Word of God.

Information-sharing should not be the only purpose of Sunday Schools; transformation of individuals through discipleship should be the goal. This requires caring teachers who have a call on their lives, and who are willing to train themselves in modern teaching methods that take into account the true nature of today's learners.

We must begin with two questions. First, what is Christian education? Secondly what is the purpose of Christian education? I came across one definition of Christian education that impressed me greatly: Christian education is a Bible-based, Holy Spirit-empowered, Christ-centered teaching-learning process. In terms of purpose, I like this definition: The purpose of Christian Education is to guide individuals at all levels of growth through contemporary teaching methodologies in order to equip them for effective ministry.

Sunday School's ultimate purpose is to produce transformed lives. This transformation does not happen accidentally, it requires a strategy. The teacher should model Jesus Christ, the Master educator, and follow His directive to make disciples.

The Sunday School training seminar in New York City was a special attempt to address this great need for Christian education among North America's Asian immigrants. I spent the day discussing the theory and practice of Christian education as it pertains to today's teens with a group of teachers. Although it was important to discuss theology, educational psychology, and pedagogy, ultimately we looked at Jesus the Master Teacher who always emphasized the pupil. He was a teacher of great authority and profound simplicity, who taught with definite goals and always started with the pupils' needs.

Jesus used a variety of teaching methods, such as questions, discussions, lectures, stories, and teaching aids. I challenged the teachers in New York to study and think creatively to find contemporary applications of Jesus' methods of teaching, and I would like to challenge all readers of this volume to consider the importance of improving Christian education for teens.

Teaching teenagers necessitates that the teacher understand their physical, mental, social, and spiritual characteristics. Physically, teens deal with bursts of energy and recurring fatigue because they grow and develop at a rapid pace. They feel awkward about their bodies and their disproportionate growth. Teenagers also have keen minds and are often critical of everyone and everything as they begin to evaluate truth about the world for themselves. Teens experience mood swings and are given to daydreaming. Socially, they are greatly influenced by their peers, with a particular awareness of the opposite sex, whom they try to impress. They are in the process of transferring loyalty from their parents to peers. Although they may act otherwise, teens especially need acceptance from teachers, who are very important to them. Teens generally look to younger adults as role models. They are also sincere and serious about their spiritual life; they possess a desire to know God, but need guidance. Teenagers cannot handle long boring lectures; rather, they prefer learning activities that will enhance their spiritual development through social interactions. The following is a short list of activities in which teens would enthusiastically involve themselves.

Possible Activities/Methods for Teens
- Word Puzzles
- Mime
- Skits
- Role Playing
- Interviews
- Debates
- Brainstorming
- Buzz Groups
- Panel Discussions
- Paraphrasing Class Discussion
- Creating News Stories
- Writing Parables
- Music

TEACHING FOR DAILY DECISIONS

Although Christian conversion is an internal matter, the Christian life displays external evidence. The New Testament documents biographies of individuals whose lives were transformed by an encounter with Jesus. The Samaritan woman who met Jesus at the well was changed by that encounter (John 4:39), and the demoniac who met Jesus received a sound mind (Luke 8:35). Similarly, the despised tax collector Zacchaeus became a philanthropist as he met Jesus in Jericho (Luke 19:8). The story of the Ethiopian eunuch testifies that an encounter with Jesus through the mediation of an evangelist is as powerful as an encounter with Jesus in the flesh. Philip introduced the Ethiopian to Jesus on a desert road in Gaza. The eunuch accepted Christ, was baptized in water in the desert, and went home rejoicing (Acts 8:38)! In the same manner, the jailor who imprisoned Paul and Silas accepted Christ and was instantly transformed. His sins were washed in the blood of the Lamb and he washed the wounds of the apostles (Acts 16:33-34)! The largest portion of the New Testament was written by Paul the persecutor who met Jesus and became the persecuted.

The change that Jesus facilitates in the lives of believers normally manifests in the decisions and choices they make. This is where Christian education becomes significant. Christian education must equip Christians to make decisions and choices that will glorify God. A Christian must exhibit a lifestyle that is different from that of a non-Christian. Ultimately, an individual's lifestyle is the outcome of the decisions and choices he or she makes. The Bible gives examples of good and bad decisions and choices. For example, Cain made a bad decision to worship with a wrong motive (Gen. 4). Esau decided to sell his birthright (Gen. 25:29-34), and Samson chose to confess the secret of his strength to Delilah (Judg. 16:15-17). King Saul decided to disobey God and keep the enemy alive (1 Sam. 15:20). The rich young ruler decided to walk away from the invitation given by Jesus (Matt. 19:16-22). Demas decided to forsake Paul because he chose to love the world (2 Tim. 4:10), and Governor Felix chose not to make a decision for Christ (Acts 24:24-26).

Thankfully, the Bible presents clear instructions about the healthy choices we must make. We are to choose unity rather than division (Ps. 133:1). Forgiveness is a better choice than bitterness (Matt. 6:12), and we must choose holiness rather than worldliness (1 Pet. 1:16). Love is a better choice than hatred (1 John 4:7-8), and healing is a better choice than brokenness (John 5:6).

Psychologists were not the first ones to say that happiness is a choice; the Bible also teaches this principle. The apostle Paul pleads with the Philippian believers to choose happiness, saying "Rejoice in the Lord always. I will say it again: Rejoice!" (Phil. 4:4). In the Old Testament, Joshua made the most important decision: "We will serve the Lord" (Josh. 24:15).

Many churchgoers are simply cultural Christians. They remind me of the Hindus in India, who are cultural Hindus and nothing more. It is the duty of Christian educators to raise the level of biblical literacy and Christian discipleship in our churches. Seminary professors have noticed an astounding level of biblical illiteracy in incoming seminary students, which appears to be a national problem. The remedy can only spring out of the local church, which must raise up disciples of Jesus who know the Word of God so well that they are able to evaluate their culture and make truly Christian decisions on a daily basis. Sometimes the word "decision" in the Charismatic vocabulary is limited to the decision to accept Christ, but we must train people for lifelong decisions. The church must equip believers to make morally right decisions. Only competent, Spirit-filled Christian education can accomplish this awesome task.

TYPES OF FAITH

Charles Farah, former professor of Theology at Oral Roberts University, discussed several types of faith in believers. He did not call his model "Stages of Faith," because he felt that they were not in a hierarchy. The first type is *historical faith*. For example, a person claims to be a Baptist because his grandparents were Baptists, but he possesses no deeper reasons for his claim. Next is *temporary faith,* which is evident in people who become excited about a spiritual experience for a short time and then lose their enthusiasm. Instead of moving from grace to grace, these individuals go from crusade to crusade. The third type of faith is *saving faith*. When a person repents and accepts Christ as Savior he experiences saving faith. The fourth category of faith is called *faith for miracles*. This type of faith is not a gift of God; rather it is something the person must "work up." The fifth type, *gift faith,* is listed among the gifts of the Spirit in 1 Corinthians 12. The next type, presented as a fruit of the Spirit in Galatians, is called *Fruit faith*. Farah calls the final type of faith *ministry faith*. He asserts that every believer is given a measure of faith according to Romans 12. This is the faith to minister to others in whatever capacity God has called us to minister. A true disciple should function at this level of faith.

The best type of faith is not faith which simply ministers to us; according to Farah, it is the faith that makes us reach out to others. This concept holds significant implications for the ministry of education in the church. Christians must be taught to live out their discipleship through teaching, training, and modeling. Christian education should enable believers to understand their faith to the degree that they can apply it in their daily lives, as they walk in the path of Christ through the power of the Holy Spirit.

THEOLOGICAL REFLECTION

A very old man and an infant are brought to a hospital at the same time with a severe asthma attack. Both need assistance in breathing, but the hospital only has one respiratory machine. If you were the doctor responsible to decide which patient should receive the only machine available, who would you give the machine to? The infant has her entire life before her, and the old man has lived a long time already. How would you make that decision as a Spirit-filled Christian?

A rich man, who has several living children, dies and leaves some artificially created embryos behind, in frozen condition, for future development. His wife wants to develop the embryos into children after the man has been dead for a while, but the living children are against the idea because they will have to share their inheritance with the children to be developed from the embryos. Should the mother be allowed to carry out her plan, or should the embryos be destroyed?

A cancer patient cannot take the pain of the disease anymore. A doctor is willing to help her become free from the pain through suicide. How would you respond to this doctor if you were a doctor or nurse working with him?

These are no longer hypothetical situations; they are real life situations brought to us by rapidly advancing technology. The same modern science that brought us satellite communication and video entertainment has also created these very difficult ethical dilemmas. How should we respond and make decisions regarding these situations as Spirit-led Christians?

There was a time when we could look for a proof text from scripture to find an answer. The Word of God is still the same; it still contains the answers to all human situations, but we no longer have the luxury of simply finding a random verse to apply to various complex situations. For instance, the Bible does not say, "Thou shall not watch MTV (vulgar music television)" or "Thou shall not commit assisted suicide."

There are still many Christians, particularly Pentecostals, who insist that a proof text can be found to solve every problem. They will often take verses out of context in order to argue their points. Although there are plenty of clear directives and commands given in God's Word, many of the dilemmas facing modern believers come in subtle and complex forms. Simplistic solutions will not clearly address the issues in these situations.

The discipline of theological reflection is needed to help believers find answers for difficult questions. Theological reflection is the spiritual discipline of looking at any experience or cultural situation through the prism of God's Word, illuminated by the Holy Spirit working within history, tradition, and a community of faith. This is a fancy way to say that in order to know what to do in a difficult and unclear situation we must seek the teaching of the Word of God and the guidance of the Holy Spirit. We should not simply look for verses to quote, but rather, we should listen to the principles and wholesome directives of the Word of God that can assist us in making decisions that will please the Lord.

God has not left us alone; He has promised to be with us as the Living Word, who has given us the written Word. He has also made us members of His body where we can depend on one another. Therefore, instead of using proof text in isolation, we must seek the will of God in prayer, reflection, and meditation, and consult with the people of God. God will reveal His will to us through His Word, His Spirit, and His people.

Theological reflection is not for the impatient. Unless a believer receives a word of wisdom or knowledge from the Holy Spirit, it takes time to discern the will of God in difficult situations. To do this well, one must study the Word of God regularly and know what is written in the Word. Only those who know what is in the Word can look for words, metaphors, images, and directives that inform and guide in the decision making process.

God's direction for certain issues is given directly in the Bible; however, for many modern dilemmas the answer must be discerned through theological reflection. On the occasions that immediate answers are required, the Holy Spirit can give us the gifts of the Spirit, such as the Word of Wisdom and the Word of Knowledge.

Certain historic Christian churches, which do not claim to be Charismatic, possess a long history of theological reflection. Conversely, Pentecostals who claim to be Spirit-filled are not known for their discipline of theological reflection. Lack of theological reflection is the fault of the believer, not the Holy Spirit. We are the ones who need to practice the disciplines of prayer, reflection, and meditation. Christian education is not an elective ministry; consistent study of the Word of God is the most important prerequisite for theological reflection. It must become a vital part of all churches and ministries. Churches must prepare Spirit-filled Christians to answer the complicated questions posed to them by modern civilization. As believers learn to reflect on God's Word, through the leading of the Holy Spirit, they will discover the divine solutions to the challenging issues that are facing them today.

CHURCH AS A THEOLOGICAL SEMINARY

The relationship between the local church and the education of future ministers has generated much discussion. Traditional seminaries and Bible colleges have been under attack for their lack of connection with the local church. Seminaries throughout the world are dealing with this issue and proposing changes to deal with it. The School of Theology and Missions at Oral Roberts University has made significant changes in its curriculum and academic procedures to ensure that the seminary and the churches influence one another. Committees of faculty members and local pastors continue to study the issue and present proposals to the faculty as a whole for final decisions. For example, modular degree programs for working pastors and fast track programs for leaders of major ministries were created as a result of this process. The seminary is becoming the primary training ground of Charismatic ministers in the new century.

Some have called for the elimination of traditional seminaries, which offer accredited theological education. I believe that accredited theological education is important, but seminaries and local churches should attempt a joint effort to provide the best training possible. I am of the opinion that the local church should provide the basic level of theological training to all future ministers. All Christians need theological education, because many are confused about what they believe. Their confusion will only increase as New Agers continue to adopt traditionally Christian terminology to mean totally different things. Only intentional and systematic study of the Bible and theology will equip believers to recognize false gods and doctrines. Although seminaries can be a great resource for the local church in this matter, the church must take responsibility to provide such training. Those who plan for full-time professional Christian ministry must seek further education in Bible colleges and seminaries.

Author and theological educator, Carnegie Samuel Calian, in *The Ideal Seminary,* shares similar sentiments. He states,

> Theological wisdom is above all a gift to the learned and unlearned by the grace of God. Realizing once again that we are all recipients of God's grace should especially humble those of us who are theological educators. The reality is that the academic degrees earned by us and issued through our schools do not necessarily guarantee that our faith has grown. This is a paradox that faces all of us who are engaged in theological education. We operate our schools, teach, write our books, and seek accreditation as if it all depends on us, the stakeholders, when in reality it all depends on the Spirit of God who imparts divine wisdom that empowers us to fulfill our destiny and equips us with a message of hope for a society in search of its soul.[9]

I share this issue to point out the importance of Christian education in the local church, not to attack academic theological education. The church cannot afford to fail in this regard because it will not survive such a failure. Calian called theological faculty to become students again in order to improve the quality of seminary teaching. Similarly, I call pastors to become students again for the purpose of becoming better teachers. According to Calian, when faculty members become students again, the following good things will happen:
1. They will value diversity more.
2. They will no longer be lecture-bound.
3. They will provide more opportunities for students to learn experientially.
4. They will use diverse materials, such as case studies, computer networking, video films, tapes, drama,

readings, and students' past experiences to create exciting teachable moments.
5. They will employ more team teaching.

I wish the same for the local churches and pastors.

CHAPTER 8

THE HEALING MINISTRY IN THE NEW CENTURY

Jesus commissioned His disciples to preach, teach, and heal. Healing has been part of the Gospel from the very beginning and, in spite of controversies throughout the ages it has remained a significant function and ministry of the Christian Church. As excellent books on the history of healing are now available, I will not attempt to present a historical defense of the healing ministry here. My focus is the biblical, theological, and practical aspects of healing.

Healing, according to the Bible, involves wholeness. Wholeness is the opposite of brokenness, which represents the condition of fallen humanity. While the secular concept of healing can be reduced to a condition without symptoms of illness or disease, the biblical concept represents wellness, balance, and harmony. The Old Testament idea of *Shalom (*peace) and the New Testament idea of *Soteria* (salvation) both represent wholeness.

We were created as whole persons in the image and likeness of God, but sin brought brokenness and alienation from God into our lives. God's ultimate plan for fallen humanity is that we would be restored and reconciled to

Him. To be whole is to be in sound condition, well, happy, prosperous, and peaceful. Wholeness happens through Jesus Christ, as He restores all that was lost through Adam (Rom. 5:17-21; 2 Cor. 5:17-21). Jesus came to seek and to save (Luke 19:10), to "preach good news to the poor . . . to proclaim freedom for the prisoners and recovery of sight for the blind" (Luke 4:18). Healing was Jesus' mission.

The Bible clearly expresses God's intention to heal His people in both the Old and New Testaments. God's nature bears witness that healing is His good pleasure. God the healer (Exod. 15:26) loved us (John 3:16) and gave Himself for us. "Surely he took our infirmities and carried our sorrows . . . and by his wounds we are healed," says Isaiah about the suffering servant (Isa. 53:4-5). Believers are advised to call the elders of the church when they are sick so that they can receive anointing with oil and prayer for their healing (James 5:13-16).

Jesus healed the sick during His earthly ministry, and He is the same yesterday, today and forever (Heb. 13:8). However, healing of the body was not the only concern Jesus had while He lived on earth; He still desires to heal all areas of our lives—body, mind, spirit, relationships, and every other aspect. Paul emphasizes this truth in 1 Thessalonians as he says, "May your whole spirit, soul and body be kept blameless at the coming of our Lord Jesus Christ" (1 Thess. 5:23). Well-being and wholeness is God's will for humankind and He has facilitated this through the life, death, resurrection, and ascension of Jesus Christ.

The Bible mentions several methods of healing, including calling for the elders, anointing with oil, the laying on of hands, and prayer. Jesus himself ministered healing in many ways. He healed by pronouncing a word (John 5:8), by touching people (Matt. 8:15), and by praying, as He did at the tomb of Lazarus (John 11:41-42).

There is a record that He occasionally used spittle (Mark 7:33) or instructed individuals to act certain ways by faith (John 5:8). On other occasions He healed individuals whose loved ones came to Jesus on their behalf (Matt. 8:10-13). Paul's words concerning the Lord's Supper in his first letter to the Corinthians seem to imply that the sacraments have a healing capacity (1 Cor. 11:27-32). According to scripture, God is a good God (Ps. 118:1) who is the giver of all good gifts (James 1:17). It is not accidental that healing is listed among the gifts of the Spirit in 1 Corinthians (1 Cor. 12:7-11).

The very design of the human body suggests that our welfare is important to God because we are fearfully and wonderfully made. Modern science is amazed at mankind's built-in immune system that not only prevents illnesses, but also has the power to cure diseases. It is no wonder the Church has confessed the healing power of Jesus' Name for two thousand years, since we are designed to be well. The scriptures, the apostolic fathers, and the entire history of the Church bear witness to God's power and His willingness to heal. We have no reason not to believe in healing and divine health.

The preventive health principles found in the Old Testament present persuasive evidence for the modern person that it is God's will for human beings to be healthy. For instance, the Old Testament recommends sanitation (Exod. 29:14), cleansing (Lev. 15), isolation (Num. 5:4), hygiene (Lev. 11), dietary regulations (Lev. 11), physical exercise (Gen. 3:19), and rest (Exod. 20:8-11). As the following passages illustrate, health and healing receive significant attention in the Bible. "I will take away sickness from among you" (Exod. 23:25); "A righteous man may have many troubles, but the Lord delivers him from them all" (Ps. 34:19); "Who forgives all your sins and heals all your diseases" (Ps. 103:3); "He sent forth his word and healed them; he rescued them from the grave" (Ps. 107:20). Many Old Testament figures experienced healing: Miriam was healed of leprosy (Num. 12:12-15), scores of people looked upon the serpent of brass in the wilderness and were healed of venomous snakebites (Num. 21:9), Naaman was healed of leprosy (2 Kings 5:1-15), and Job received healing from deadly sores (Job 42:10-13).

Various forms of healing occur in Scripture. In the Old Testament, many barren women were healed, and several people were raised from the dead. The New Testament also documents a cloud of witnesses who received healing through the ministry of Jesus. Healing accounts in Scripture did not end with Jesus' ministry; healing continued throughout the lives of the apostles. Scores of individuals in the New Testament received healing through the ministry of the apostles.

FAITH AND HEALING

The relationship between faith and healing is often debated and unclear in many church traditions. As a result, people are sometimes blamed for not receiving their healing and accused of not having enough faith. This pattern of blaming the sick is not supported by the Word of God.

Faith has been defined as seeing the invisible, believing the incredible, and accomplishing the impossible. According to the Bible, those who come to God must believe that He is, and that He rewards those who diligently seek Him (Heb. 11:6). Faith is listed among the gifts of the Spirit, as well as among the fruits of the Spirit, and Jesus related faith to healing on many occasions (Matt. 8:10, 13; 9:22, 29; Mark 5:34; 10:52). Although He rebuked individuals with little faith (Matt. 14:31; Mark 4:40; Luke

8:25), it was generally not in relation to healing. In Matthew 17, Jesus named unbelief as one factor hindering deliverance and recommended fasting and prayer.

The Bible refers to at least six modes of healing: (1) due to the patient's faith, (2) due to the faith of those who brought the patient to Jesus, (3) due to anointing and laying on of hands, (4) due to confession, (5) through casting out of spirits, and (6) through miracles. The Bible also speaks of different dimensions of faith, such as a measure of faith (Rom. 12:3) and fullness of faith (Acts 6:5, 8; 11:24). Faith comes by hearing (Rom. 10:17), faith justifies (Rom. 5:1), purifies (Acts 15:9), and sanctifies (Acts 26:18). We must live by faith (Rom. 1:17), walk by faith (2 Cor. 5:7), work by faith (2 Thess. 1:11), overcome by faith (1 John 5:4), pray by faith (James 5:15), and be healed by faith (Acts 14:9).

Although faith is a necessary element for an individual to be healed, the burden of faith is not on the patient but on the community of faith. It is wonderful when the patient believes; however, when he or she is weak or lacking in faith the community should not waste time blaming or accusing this individual. Instead, it should rise up, stand in the gap, and declare like the Apostle Paul in the endangered ship: "For I (we) believe God."

Oral Roberts Ministries is a global ministry founded by Oklahoma healing evangelist Oral Roberts, who was healed from tuberculosis in his youth. I have been part of this ministry for over two decades. Oral Roberts is the founder and chancellor of Oral Roberts University, which grew out of the fires of healing evangelism that enveloped America and many other nations a few decades ago. Millions of people attended the healing crusades conducted by Oral Roberts, which were held in massive tents across America and other nations. Thousands of individuals reported that they were healed from various types of illnesses at these meetings. Roberts preached the simple message that God is a good God, and that He wants to heal people. In spite of much persecution, primarily from denominational Christians, his message resonated well with people in need across the world. The tent ministry evolved into a television ministry that continues today through the healing ministry of his son, the current president of Oral Roberts University, Richard Roberts. A healing service entitled *Something Good Tonight*, hosted by President Richard and Lindsay Roberts, airs daily from the ORU campus. Their ministry receives numerous medically documented healing testimonies annually.

Oral Roberts is foremost among the healing evangelists of the twentieth century. As America's pioneer healing evangelist, he still travels and ministers throughout America. Several evangelists are well known today for their healing ministries. Benny Hinn, who believes that Kathryn Kuhlman's mantle has fallen on him and Richard Roberts, are prominent among them. God seems to use some of His servants to minister healing to His people to a greater extent than He uses others.

Pastors and evangelists who minister healing must encourage people to believe God with all their hearts, because faith pleases God (Heb. 11:6). It is important that ministers understand Oral Roberts's teaching on the releasing of one's faith through a point of contact. The act of releasing one's faith to God, rather than the point of contact itself, is the important aspect of this teaching. Jesus taught, "Everything is possible for him who believes" (Mark 9:23); "And these signs will accompany those who believe" (Mark 16:17).

SIGNS AND WONDERS

Oral Roberts University School of Theology and Missions is called a Signs and Wonders Seminary because the administration and faculty believe that the Holy Spirit is at work in the world today as He was during the first century. The Holy Spirit still performs signs and wonders as in the days of the apostles. We teach courses such as *Holy Spirit in the Now* and *Signs and Wonders,* in order to investigate this thesis and to train Spirit-filled ministers to expect the move of the Holy Spirit in their own ministries.

Howard Ervin, the most senior professor in the School of Theology and Missions, recently published a definitive work on healing entitled *Healing: Sign of the Kingdom.* This title summarizes the testimony of the faculty at ORU's Seminary. A biblical scholar of great repute, Ervin concludes that signs and wonders still follow the preaching of the Gospel; they confirm the good news. God does not perform miracles to entertain believers, but as a sign to the unbelievers to confirm His Word. Signs and wonders manifest the power of the Kingdom of God, but Ervin discourages believers from merely seeking signs. Believers should learn the mysteries of the Kingdom of God through the teachings of Jesus so they can live as disciples engaged in Kingdom business.

Portions of the foreword I composed for Ervin's book are given below, as they shed some light on the issue at hand.

> In *Healing: Sign of the Kingdom,* Professor Howard Ervin reflects biblically and theologically on the healing ministry of Jesus and the apostles. Reflecting deeply on his study of the relevant biblical passages, as well as on his

own experiences and keen observations, Ervin comes up with an affirming biblical foundation for a healing ministry in contemporary society. Ervin sees healing as a vital part of Jesus' tri-fold ministry of preaching, teaching, and healing. Healing is a sign of the Kingdom of God; it manifests the power of God's reign.

Signs follow the proclamation of the Gospel and they confirm the message of the Kingdom of God. Signs are for the unbelievers. Believers do not need signs, but they can receive healing as gifts of love from their Father ...

The Gospels contain three categories of healing miracles: by the spoken word, by physical touch, and by use of material substance. Divine healing is not limited to physical healing; it involves all aspects of a person. Healing is wholeness. Ervin affirms deliverance ministry and establishes that the biblical worldview, unlike the worldview of the Enlightenment, is a multidimensional view where spirit and matter form a continuum . . . . According to Ervin, the faith that heals is the faith that saves, and the faith that saves is the faith that heals.

I believe that both Ervin's affirmation and caution are valid. We should have healing services for believers and expect that miracles will happen as signs to the unbelievers. We need to train church members to move beyond the level of seeking signs to maintain their faith. The words of the book of Hebrews apply to us today:

In fact, though by this time you ought to be teachers, you need someone to teach you the elementary truths of God's Word all over again. You need milk, not solid food! Anyone who lives on milk, being still an infant, is not acquainted with the teaching about righteousness. But solid food is for the mature, who by constant use have trained themselves to distinguish good from evil (Heb. 5:12-14).

EVANGELISTIC VERSUS PASTORAL HEALING

I believe that there are evangelistic and pastoral approaches to healing. People who do not recognize this distinction seem to attack one form or the other. The truth is that both, when conducted under the guidance of the Holy Spirit, are valid forms of healing ministry. We need to recognize that God in His wisdom gave the Church apostles, prophets, evangelists, pastors, and teachers. Not all of the needs of His body can be met by individuals in one particular function of ministry; all offices are needed to equip the saints for the work of service.

God frequently uses evangelists to minister healing to His people. Evangelists often do not develop the same type of relationship with the individuals to whom they minister that a pastor must have. The ministry of evangelism is based on the needs of people and focused on evangelistic preaching. The evangelist may apply any of the biblical methods for healing because God honors His Word and heals the sick. Pastoral care, however, is a field that deals with the relational aspect of healing ministry. Pastors are shepherds called by God to care for His people, and they have a unique relationship with the people under their care. Although they may use the same biblical healing methods as the evangelists, the relational dynamic will play a role in the healing process.

According to theologians Williams Clebsch and Charles Jaekle, the ministry of pastoral care deals with healing, guiding, sustaining, and reconciling.[1] Thomas Oden, professor of Theology at Drew University, also considers it a ministry of listening, understanding, and comforting.[2] Pastors must practice what is called the incarnational presence ministry. The minister seeks to be intentionally present with the individual in need as if Christ Himself is present with him. Pastors may also occasionally have to confront people through a ministry called *carefrontation,* in which one must speak truth in love. Here one would point out, in a confidential and loving way, some of the problems or lifestyle issues contributing to an individual's illness, if that person is seeking healing.

The focus of pastoral healing ministry is prayer. According to a model developed at Oral Roberts University, pastoral healing ministry includes the following steps: *Incarnational Presence, Listening, Information Gathering, Prayer,* and *Referral. Follow up* may also be a part of this model.

Ted Estes, a pastor in Claremore, Oklahoma, studied the John Wimber model of healing for his Doctor of Ministry research project at Oral Roberts University. He practices a model with the following steps: *Interview, Clarification and Diagnostic Decision, Prayer Selection, Prayer,* and *Reflection.* Father Francis MacNutt, a Charismatic healing minister and former Catholic priest, practices what is called Soaking Prayer, which involves laying on of hands and continuing focused prayer for persons with serious illnesses.

THEOLOGICAL PRESUPPOSITIONS

As presented in my previous work on pastoral care, *Ministry Between Miracles,* a pastoral ministry of healing is based on certain presuppositions.[3] The first assumption is that health and illness are both dynamic in nature. Health is not merely the absence of illness, but a wholeness of being. Wholeness is the aspect of human nature that defies fragmentation in body, mind, and spirit.

A second assumption is that human beings are unitary. In other words, the human body, mind, and spirit are "fearfully and wonderfully" interwoven at profoundly deep levels. Each aspect of human life interacts with and influences every other aspect, which means that when one part of a person is hurting he hurts throughout his body, mind, and spirit.

This leads to a third assumption that the individual is able, knowingly or unknowingly, to affect his or her own state of wellness or illness. Personal attitudes, habits of discipline, priorities, and choices are significantly related to one's wholeness or lack of health. The faith or personal theology of an individual is a potential resource for health or a hindrance to wellness. For example, one individual's theology may burden him with guilt and condemnation, while another individual's theology sets him free from condemnation.

A Spirit-led ministry of pastoral healing is based on additional theological presuppositions:

- God is a good God and He wants us to be whole. The New Testament word *soteria*, like the Old Testament word *shalom*, connotes salvation, healing, preservation, and harmony in relationships.

- God is the source of *all* healing. Whether healing results from medical intervention, faith-filled thoughts and prayer, natural biological restorative processes, or a combination of these, all healing comes from God. Growing up in a Pentecostal church that did not rely much on medical healing, I personally found this teaching of Oral Roberts to be revelatory and freeing.
- Divine intervention in the lives of individuals in need is always a real possibility. This cannot be guaranteed for each person in terms of time and place, but it can certainly be expected. A minister can sincerely pray for divine interventions or miracles, and it is safe to assume that God can and may intervene at any point to bring about the kind of healing that He wants in any particular situation. This is why the New Testament commands us to pray and have faith for healings.
- Healing takes various forms. Sometimes healing comes instantaneously and at other times it comes more gradually. Sometimes healing comes as a consequence of medical intervention and sometimes as a result of prayer.
- Healing is for wholeness, not for perfection. True wholeness, because it involves body, mind, and spirit, issues from a Christ-centered life of discipleship.
- Wholeness involves every aspect of one's life: physical, spiritual, emotional, relational, economic, and environmental.
- There is a reality called the fullness of time (*kairos*). Healing occurs in the fullness of time.
- Healing is enhanced by the things that nourish the spirit, such as love (1 John 4:7), hope (Ps. 42:5, 11),

- faith (Matt. 9:22), the will to live (John 5:6), and laughter (Phil. 4:4).
- The body of Christ is entrusted with the ministry of healing and must guard against inadvertently promoting illness.
- Pastoral counseling is extended altar ministry.
- Christian love heals. The miracle that changed the life of the Samaritan woman was that Jesus accepted her even though He knew everything she had ever done (John 4:29).
- Caring heals. True caring happens when one is willing to give up one's own agenda to consider the agenda of another, as Christ did when He gave himself for us (Phil. 2:6, 7).
- Persons engaged in the healing ministry of Jesus must consider that their own divinely formed nature is a sign and wonder of God.

Pastoral healing ministry is an extension of the ministry of Jesus. In a place of pain, such as a hospital, a minister must represent the presence of Jesus. Inhabited by the life-giving Spirit of Jesus, a minister can be an incarnational presence to hurting people, a "living reminder of Jesus;" as Henri Nouwen would say, he is an individual whose life reminds others of Jesus of Nazareth. Motivated by God's love and enabled by His Spirit, a caregiver becomes a channel of God's grace. As he or she ministers in the Name of Christ, this grace impacts other people's lives.

A minister of the Gospel has certain resources at his disposal. Primary among these resources is the minister's own identity as a person saved by the grace of God and filled with the Holy Spirit. William Hulme describes other powerful resources, including prayer, faith, sacraments, scripture, counseling skills, and the Christian community.[4]

One can rely on personal resources and pastoral authority to establish healing relationships. The Holy Spirit will work in and through these relationships to bring healing and wholeness to persons.

HEALING IN THE LOCAL CHURCH

The local church of the twenty-first century should be a healing place. Although our world is more secularized and generally hostile to religion in many ways, discussion of spiritual matters is more acceptable today. Research on the impact of prayer and meditation on cardiac patients, nuns, and Buddhist monks has opened even the secular mind to the power of prayer; albeit, any type of prayer. The Church should take advantage of this openness to teach people about faith in Jesus Christ and prayer in the Name of Jesus. Many people coming to the churches are wounded and fragmented; therefore, the church must offer them more than a message on positive thinking. We have something powerful to offer people for the healing of body, mind, spirit, finances, and relationships. Much of what the church offers is preventive. Preventive teaching on moral commandments and instructions concerning the care and discipline of the body are important contributions for maintaining physical healing. Opportunities for forgiveness in relationships, the development of the fruits of the Spirit, and the possibility of renewing one's mind are very important preventive measures for maintaining healing of the mind. The good news of eternal life, opportunities to worship, the gifts of the Spirit, the resources of the community of faith and the privilege of prayer are contributions the church can make for spiritual well-being.

The church possesses many resources for its curative work, including the utilization of the elders of the church to anoint the sick and pray for them, the sacraments as instruments of healing, professional as well as pastoral counseling, instruction in whole person lifestyle, prayer partners and altar counselors, healing services, hospital ministry, and even on-going healing schools. The church can sponsor healing crusades inside and outside of its walls, and can invite evangelists to minister to the people. Pastors and evangelists working together can enhance the ministry of healing in the local church. Healing crusades provide evangelistic opportunities as people hear the Gospel and see the power of the Spirit manifesting in signs, wonders, and miracles. The local church must support missionary evangelists and healing ministers, in order to expand the ministry of the church to the community and the world.

Unfortunately, there are still churches that do not teach about the healing ministry of Jesus. There are others that talk about it but never practice it. The new century calls for churches that will teach and practice healing ministry. Our world desperately needs healing, and many in the churches are also hurting badly. The church should not wait for medical doctors to do all the healing work; ministers and physicians must compliment each other's work. I am very grateful to Oral Roberts for his pioneering work in merging medicine and prayer at the former City of Faith Medical and Research Center in Tulsa, Oklahoma. Doctors, nurses, and ministers worked hand-in-hand at the City of Faith to bring healing to patients who had come from all over the world. Roberts pioneered the concept of healing teams that included doctors, nurses, ministers, and other professionals. As a Pentecostal/Charismatic, he was open to the contributions of the medical field, and at the same time he believed in the power of the Holy Spirit to bring healing and wholeness to people. As a chaplain and prayer partner at the hospital in the 1980s, I witnessed the power of the Holy Spirit working though these healing teams.

Although the City of Faith closed, physicians who were trained there still spread the message of whole person healing throughout the world. Many medical schools and hospitals are now practicing what was taught at the City of Faith concerning whole person healing; these ideas were considered novel when the City of Faith implemented them. At a time when Pentecostals and Charismatics were hostile toward medicine, Oral Roberts had the courage to declare that all healing is from God. His bold stand freed a great number of Pentecostals to receive healing regardless of the avenue through which it came. May his legacy of whole person healing continue through the graduates of Oral Roberts University, and particularly through the churches and ministries of the graduates of ORU School of Theology and Missions.

CHAPTER 9

POWER-FILLED SERVANT LEADERSHIP

Much misunderstanding exists in the body of Christ concerning ministry. Often our perceptions of ministry are based on our personal experiences with ministers and, unfortunately, not all such experiences are positive. Our perceptions of ministry should come from the Word of God, and help us recognize that it is God who makes ministers. Bible colleges and seminaries cannot call people into the ministry; they can only train people whom God calls.

Ministry does not depend on the natural talents of ministerial candidates. God can use our strengths and our weaknesses, and He calls whom He pleases. The truth is that all of us are called to be disciples, and as disciples of Christ, we are all called to minister. Some of us are called to full-time Christian service, while others might carry out their life's work as a service to God.

When God called Moses, Moses did not present his qualifications to God; he acknowledged that he could not speak eloquently. Jeremiah presented his inability to speak as an excuse, and when God called Saul to be the first king of Israel, he recognized his humble origin. None of these individuals claimed their competence, yet today we seem to think of people with talent as the best candidates for ministry. God-given talents have their place in ministry, but talents do not make the real difference; God's call and an individual's obedience to that call are the crucial factors in effective ministry.

Paul the apostle makes it very clear that ministry is service. He uses the term "servant" or "slave" to describe himself, stating that he is a servant of the Lord, a servant of the church, and a servant of the Gospel. Ministry is servant leadership that involves offering service to God and man. Spirit-filled ministry is servant leadership empowered by the Holy Spirit.

Many have written about the topic of Christian leadership. According to Bruce Goettsche, Christian leaders have the following characteristics: they love people, they have a servant attitude, they are honest, they think big, they fight for the ones in need, they build people up, and they give the best they have.[1] All Christian leaders can adopt these good qualities; the challenge, however, is to be a Spirit-filled servant leader.

NEXT STAGE OF LEADERSHIP

Even the secular world is pointing out the need for behavioral change among leaders. For example, changes are taking place in the area of non-profit leadership. According to Warren Bennis and Burt Nanus, in their book *Leaders: The Strategy for Taking Charge*, non-profit leadership is entering a new stage. They list the following areas of change:

From	To
Having few leaders at the top	Having leaders at every level
Leading by goal setting	Leading through vision
Seeking efficiency	Seeking effectiveness
Adopting change	Anticipating change
Hierarchal administration	Collegial administration
Directing and supervising	Empowering and inspiring teams
Information held by a few	Information shared within and outside the organization
Bossing	Coaching
Developing administrators	Developing leaders[2]

NEW PARADIGM

In his book *The Young Evangelicals,* Robert Webber of Northern Baptist Theological Seminary in Lombard, Illinois talks about a new paradigm of church and leadership. According to Webber, the church should be a community that prefers relationship to anonymity.[3] This implies that Christian worship must evolve from a mere program to actual interaction and from constraint to expression. Spirituality must change from obedience to external things to living by internal convictions, and values must alter from secular to Kingdom values.

Webber indicates that a change in priorities is in order. He says that pastors must move from personal power to servanthood in the area of leadership, and youth ministers must give prayer priority over parties. Similarly, evangelicals ought to value relationship building over rallies, and Christian educators must transform persons rather than just give information. Missiologists must focus more on contexts than culture, and social activists should emphasize presence over programs.

BIBLICAL LANGUAGE OF LEADERSHIP

The language of leadership in modern church circles seems to be dominated by secular concepts and models. For instance, some ministers follow an executive model in which complexity is rewarded. According to Edward B. Bratcher, in *Walk on Water Syndrome,* others follow a million dollar round table model that rewards salesmanship.[4] A third model places responsibility on the president of a corporation to keep stockholders happy, while the crowded calendar model emphasizes and rewards activity. These models appear practical but not necessarily biblical. Gordon Fee's advice, in *Gospel and Spirit,* encourages us to consider the biblical language of leadership.[5] He challenges us to review the true meaning of the following terms: church (*Ekklesia*), people (*Laos*), covenant (*Diatheke*), saints (*Hoi Hagioi*), and chosen (*Eklektos*). Fee challenges Christian leaders to consider the concepts of family (2 Cor. 6:18), household (1 Tim. 3:5, 15), body (1 Cor. 10:17), temple (1 Cor. 3:16), and commonwealth (Phil. 3:20, 21). Any definition of leadership derived from these biblical terms and concepts will have the distinctiveness of Christian servant leadership.

SECRETS OF SUCCESS

In his biography *Expect a Miracle*, Oral Roberts shares ten secrets of his success in ministry.

1. He learned that the message he carried was greater than his identity as the messenger.
2. He ensured that he was anointed each time he ministered.
3. He made it a practice to reinforce his preaching by his own personal testimony.
4. He insisted on remaining constant in his integrity and purpose.

5. He chose to work with believers who authentically believed God.
6. Through experience, he learned to identify the key issues involved in a situation. In other words, he did not major in minors.
7. He learned how to use a point of contact, which is an act that allows an individual to release his faith to accomplish God's purposes. For example, a woman who had been sick for many years reached out and touched Jesus' garment as a point of contact and was instantly healed (Mark 5:28).
8. He believed that it is possible to change methods but not principles.
9. He learned that faith is present whenever one begins to seek it.
10. He practiced sowing and reaping as a lifestyle.[6]

According to Edward B. Bratcher, ministers need certain guidelines by which to measure success. Because of the multitude of issues they experience in ministry, it is hard to see success even when there is significant progress. The following guidelines can be used to measure success:
1. Define the meaning of one's ministry.
2. Define success for oneself.
3. Break down major goals into measurable goals.
4. Avoid comparing one's ministry with the ministry of another.
5. Consider the goals of ministry, the gifts of ministry, and the context of ministry.
6. Goals must include spiritual goals.
7. Clarify the goals of the institution as opposed to one's own goals.
8. Do actual study of progress or lack thereof.

9. Have services of celebration for smaller achievements.
10. Keep a daily journal to document ongoing ministry.[7] Ministers will benefit from remembering the words of Mother Teresa, "God doesn't call us to be successful; He calls us to be faithful."

MANAGEMENT VERSUS LEADERSHIP

John Kotter, a professor at Harvard Business School, differentiates management from leadership in his book *Leading Change*. According to Kotter, management has to do with planning and budgeting, while leadership has to do with establishing direction for an organization.[8] Managers organize and staff an organization, while leaders communicate direction to people. In Kotter's view, controlling and problem solving are management duties; leaders are called to motivate and inspire followers.

CONFLICT RESOLUTION

Although ministry is God's work, it often causes conflict among people. Ministers often find themselves in the middle of such conflicts. Most ministers are not comfortable handling conflicts, so they tend to avoid or deny them. Some try to cope by belittling the problem, while others try to resolve the issue by arguing in a destructive fashion. The goal of a leader should be to approach problems in a constructive way through one of the many models of conflict resolution. The following outlines one such model developed by Kenneth O. Gangel.

1. Classify and define the problem.
2. Develop criteria for a successful solution.
3. Generate alternatives.
4. Compare alternatives to criteria.

5. Choose an alternative.
6. Implement the decision.
7. Monitor the decision and get feedback.[9]

This conflict resolution model is very similar to the problem solving model presented by John Lawyer in his book, *Communication Skills for Ministry*.
1. Identify a problem in terms of desired outcome.
2. Identify all possible options and clarify them.
3. Evaluate every option.
4. Decide on an acceptable option.
5. Develop an implementation plan which should answer the questions: What? Who? Resources? Time?
6. Develop an evaluation strategy.
7. Review the experience.[10]

LIMITS OF MINISTRY

Ministers must deal with many personal limitations in the face of unlimited demands in ministry. If a minister can develop the skill of time management, he will be able to balance the limited amount of time available to do all that is required. This involves the art of self-limitation. Ministers must also face limited energy, because ministry is never really finished. When a minister attempts to finish the work in order to gain a sense of completion, he is likely to experience a sense of failure. It is better to conserve one's energy by dealing with priorities based on one's values. Ministers also contend with the limitations of knowledge. No minister possesses knowledge of everything that needs to be known; therefore, he must be a lifelong learner, continuously improving his knowledge base. Ministers can attempt to utilize other persons as resources in the area of knowledge. For example, seminaries and Bible colleges offer educational experiences for ministers, but they can also be sources of expert knowledge for local ministries. Ministry also confronts individuals with limitations in the area of achievement; a minister cannot base his sense of well-being on accomplishments. Ministers can periodically celebrate smaller achievements to remind themselves that they are moving toward bigger goals.

EFFECTIVE LEADERSHIP

J. Robert Clinton, professor of leadership at Fuller Theological Seminary, lists seven leadership lessons he has observed emerging in his classes:

1. Effective leaders maintain a learning posture throughout life.
2. Effective leaders value spiritual authority as a primary power base.
3. Effective leaders recognize leadership selection and development as a priority function.
4. Effective leaders view relational empowerment as both a means and a goal of ministry.
5. Effective leaders who are productive over a lifetime have a dynamic ministry philosophy.
6. Effective leaders evidence a growing awareness of their sense of destiny.
7. Effective leaders increasingly perceive their ministry in terms of a lifetime perspective instead of a hit and run.[11]

Henri Nouwen also has much to say about ministry leadership. He believes that the minister, as a servant leader, is called to be a wounded healer whose wounds become a source of healing for others.[12] Yet Nouwen is careful to delineate the difference between wounded healers and bleeding healers. A bleeding healer is one who is still hurting from his own injuries and disappointments, whereas a wounded healer is in the process of advancing toward wholeness. A wounded healer carries scars, but they are not bleeding; as a result, the wounded healer is able to focus on others and minister to them. Nouwen's perspective is a sobering reminder, even to those who move in the power of the Holy Spirit, to seek personal wholeness.

According to Nouwen, a minister must be a person of prayer. No ministry can exist without prayer and the Word, because a minister must test all things by the Word of God. The Word of God is his standard for faith and conduct, since he hears the voice of the Spirit within himself. The Word of God is the currency of transaction for the minister.

For Nouwen, ministry is also hospitality. A minister makes room for strangers on the couch in his heart, and as a good host he must be comfortable with himself before his guests can feel at home. Nouwen calls the minister a living reminder of Jesus. Just as the bread and the cup of communion remind us of the life, death, and resurrection of Jesus, a minister's life, according to Nouwen, should remind people of Jesus of Nazareth. Nouwen believes that God's work is not limited to an individual's strengths; He also redeems our weaknesses and uses them for His glory. As I have mentioned earlier, Nouwen's work is missing the power dimensions of ministry; however, the leadership model he presents can be incorporated into a Spirit-empowered model of servant leadership.

A SPIRIT-LED MODEL

The Bible frequently speaks about leaders and leadership. God the Father is a leader who has led His people throughout history. God the Son invited people to discipleship saying, "Follow me," and scripture is clear that

God the Holy Spirit is also to be our leader when it says, "Be led by the Spirit."

The Bible contains a long list of godly leaders. Abraham led his family out of a pagan land, and Joseph led the government of Egypt during a period of crisis. Moses led the people of God out of Egypt, Miriam led them in worship, and Joshua led Israel into the Promised Land. Deborah, as a judge and prophetess, was also a leader of the people of God. David led as a man after God's own heart, and Elijah provided prophetic leadership. Elisha followed in Elijah's footsteps and also became a leader of prominence. Daniel was a leader with great wisdom in Babylon.

In the New Testament, Peter was a leading personality among the disciples, but Paul provided apostolic leadership to the early Church. He was an exemplary leader, who said, "Follow me as I follow Christ." Priscilla provides an example of women's ministry in the early church, and Timothy was a young pastor/leader.

Servant leadership was prominent throughout the history of the Church, beginning with the Church fathers. For example, St. Augustine, Martin Luther, John Calvin, John Wesley, Jonathan Edwards, Charles Finney, Charles Parham, William Seymour, Kathryn Kuhlman, and Martin Luther King, Jr. are only a few who have left their mark on the Church and on the world; the list is long.

Ministerial servant leadership is different from all other forms of leadership. Jesus told his disciples that they should not "lord it over" their followers as the heathen do; leadership in ministry follows the paradigm of the Kingdom of God. In God's Kingdom, the leader does not give pain, He absorbs it. The shepherd does not wound the sheep; instead, he risks his life for the sheep. Leadership in God's Kingdom is defined by the following values: The first shall be the last and the last shall be the first; giving is receiving, and dying is the way to live.

I believe that Spirit-filled servant leadership has some unique requirements. Spirit-filled leadership is service with power; we serve others in the Name of Christ in the power of the Holy Spirit. Servant leadership requires: (1) an intimate encounter with God, (2) the anointing of the Holy Spirit, and (3) willingness to take action by faith. Spirit-filled leadership is a walk by faith.

Encounter with God

All godly leaders in scripture experienced an intimate encounter with the living God. God met with Abraham personally (Gen. 17:1-6), and Moses encountered God on a mountainside in the burning bush (Exod. 3:1-7). Joshua had an experience with God after Moses died (Josh. 1:1-5), and God revealed Himself to Samuel when Samuel was a young man in the temple being discipled by Eli the priest (1 Sam. 3:4-11). Elijah encountered the Word of God as he was commanded to go and hide himself by the brook Cherith (1 Kings 17:2-3). Isaiah encountered God in the year Uzziah died (Isa. 6:1-9), and Ezekiel met with God as the Lord asked him about the dry bones in the valley (Ezek. 37:3).

An encounter with God is a life-transforming experience. Isaiah's experience demonstrates the framework of an encounter with God. First, Isaiah encounters the glory of God as He is seated high and lifted up in the temple. Immediately afterwards, Isaiah unexpectedly encounters impurity in himself. The unpleasantness of this confrontation causes him to cry out, "Woe is me. I am a man of unclean lips!" Isaiah recognizes that his position as a prophet involves the use of his tongue, which is often found to be unclean, but God does not leave him in this condition of despair. God sends an angel with a red hot coal to touch Isaiah's lips, and he is cleansed.

After the cleansing process, he has an encounter with the call of God, when God asks Isaiah, "Who will go for us? Whom shall we send?" Isaiah responds, "Here am I, send me."

Often leaders miss the second step of an encounter with God, which involves the acknowledgement of one's own inadequacies. Many overlook the mystery that God can use our weaknesses as well as our strengths. In fact, He can turn our weaknesses into strengths.

The lives of biblical leaders demonstrate that an encounter with God can truly transform a life. For instance, Abraham's life was changed in order to be a blessing to the nations, and Moses was transformed into the man who was to lead God's people out of bondage. Joshua was changed as God raised him up to lead them into the Promised Land. Samuel, Isaiah, Elijah, Ezekiel, and many others were also transformed through their encounters with the Lord.

A person's name is a significant part of his or her identity. Thus, when an individual's name is changed through an encounter with God, his or her identity is also changed. Jacob became Israel, Saul became Paul, and Simon became Peter.

An encounter with God also changes a person's agenda. The individual's goals are no longer important; he or she adopts God's goals. After the burning bush experience, Moses did not try to deliver the people his own way; he adopted God's way. The theme of a servant leader becomes, "Not my will, but thine."

Anointing of the Holy Spirit

Spirit-filled leadership requires the anointing of the Holy Spirit. Anointing here refers to the presence and power of God resting upon the leader. Personal qualities and abilities are not the most important aspects of a servant leader's work; the empowerment of the Holy Spirit makes the difference in one's service to others. The Bible clearly illustrates this point.

When King Saul disobeyed God, Samuel went to Bethlehem to anoint David as the next leader of the Israelites. Samuel invited Jesse and his sons to a place of worship (1 Sam. 16:3). Jesse's first son, Eliab, appeared to be an outstanding candidate, but the Lord said to Samuel, "Do not consider his appearance or his height . . . .The Lord does not look at the things man looks at. Man looks at the outward appearance, but the Lord looks at the heart" (1 Sam. 16:7). Samuel was surprised as God rejected each of Jesse's seven sons and asked, "Are these all the sons you have?" When Jesse mentioned his youngest son, David, Samuel told him to send for David. When David approached, Samuel heard the Lord say, "Rise, anoint him. He is the one." "So Samuel took the horn of oil and anointed him in the presence of his brothers, and from that day on the Spirit of the Lord came upon David in power" (1 Sam. 16:13). David was selected by God and anointed by Samuel; the anointing brought the power of God into David's life.

Spirit-filled ministry is a powerful ministry. The power does not stem from personal charisma, but from the power of the Holy Spirit. The *charismata*, or gifts of the Holy Spirit, are more important than personality or personal charisma. The anointing of the Holy Spirit gives the unction for service, and the Holy Spirit empowers the servant leader.

The New Testament ministers were anointed by the Holy Spirit. According to the Gospel of John, Jesus breathed on His disciples. The apostles were among the 120 who received the Holy Spirit in the upper room on the day of Pentecost. Paul, a latecomer, also received the baptism of the Holy Spirit prior to his apostolic ministry. Servant leadership is not powerless ministry; it is ministry in the power of the Holy Spirit. Such a ministry is available for every individual whom God chooses, regardless of his personal competence or charisma.

Walk by Faith

It is one thing to receive the anointing of the Holy Spirit, but it is another matter to act on it. Christian ministry is a walk of faith. This faith walk is the door that allows the Holy Spirit to manifest Himself through the life and ministry of God's servants, and it is the anointing of the Holy Spirit that leads a minister to take action by faith. The relationship between Elijah and Elisha demonstrates this concept. After Elijah trained Elisha to become a prophet, the time came for Elijah to be taken from Elisha. Elijah asked Elisha what he might do for him. Just as Solomon asked for wisdom, Elisha replied that he wanted a double portion of the Spirit that was upon Elijah. Although he could have asked for anything, Elisha asked for a double portion of the anointing. Elijah responded that if Elisha saw him depart, he would receive his wish. Elisha followed Elijah from Gilgal to Bethel, from Bethel to Jericho, and from Jericho to the Jordan River. As Elisha watched, Elijah struck the Jordan with his mantle, and the river opened up for them to cross over to the other side. Soon after the senior prophet was taken up to heaven in a chariot of fire, his mantle fell to the ground. The mantle was a symbol of the anointing that was upon Elijah. Elisha picked up the mantle and held it in his hand as he stood by the river. As he struck the river with the mantle, he asked, "Where is the God of Elijah?" Elisha had watched Elijah take many steps of faith; now the anointing that had rested upon Elijah had fallen upon him. It was time for him to act by faith.

Elisha knew Elijah's God, and he knew God's character. He recognized that Elijah's God was a God who spoke, and he understood that Elijah's God would be able to provide for all his needs. Elisha possessed the knowledge that Elijah's God could send rain or fire as needed and divide the river, but mere knowledge was not enough. He had to act on that knowledge under the anointing he had just received. As an act of pure faith, Elisha struck the water just as Elijah had, and it divided to the right and to the left! Just as faith without works is dead, so Spirit-filled servant leadership must involve walking and working by faith.

The anointing of the Holy Spirit enables the Christian minister to claim the authority that belongs to him through the power of the Holy Spirit. When a minister walks by faith, he demonstrates his trust in the words of Jesus who said, "All authority in heaven and on earth has been given to me. Therefore go . . . ." Elisha's life of obedience demonstrates the importance of taking action by faith. The river would not have opened if he had just stood and waited. Striking the river was the first step of a great and powerful ministry.

The book of Kings recounts the miracles Elisha performed. For example, when poisonous water was killing the land, Elisha cleansed it by adding salt. This miracle followed his first step of faith at the Jordan. Similarly, Elisha instructed Naaman, the deathly ill commander of the Syrian army, to immerse himself in the river seven times and Naaman was healed. This healing would not have occurred if Elisha had merely stood by the river holding the mantle in his hand. In the same manner, the widow whose sons were in danger of being enslaved received ministry and help from Elisha. She was obedient when the prophet instructed her to borrow vessels from her neighbors, and her obedience met the needs of her family. If Elisha had not taken the first step of faith in his ministry, the desperate needs of many would not have been met.

The key to success in power-filled servant leadership requires a true encounter with the living God, the anointing of the Holy Spirit, and the willingness to step out in faith. A missionary directing a Bible college in the country of India shared the following testimony. A recently converted young man enrolled as a student at the Bible school. He was newly born again, Spirit-filled, and inexperienced in ministry. As he was going by an open market one day, he saw a Hindu priest unsuccessfully attempt to cast the devil out of a young girl. As the young man passed by, he perceived God's voice in his heart saying, "You go and set that girl free." He tried to ignore the voice and kept walking, but the voice repeated that he had to go back. The priest gave him permission to pray for the young girl. The inexperienced Bible student laid his hand on the young girl and rebuked the evil spirit in the Name of Jesus; she was instantly healed. The big commotion that followed caused him to leave the scene.

This happened during a time of great tension between Hindus and Christians in the community. As a result, the young Bible school student realized that he might be the target of retaliation by Hindu extremists. The next morning he awoke to the rumbling sound of a crowd around his little house. With fear and trembling he went to the door to see what was happening, certain that the Hindus had come to attack him. As he opened the door, he was surprised to hear the people say, "We heard that a man by the name of Jesus lives in this house, and we heard that He healed a young girl in the marketplace yesterday. We want Him to come and heal these sick people too." It was not the Bible student's knowledge or expertise that broke through in that marketplace; it was his willingness to step out in faith as the Holy Spirit prompted him. He had an encounter with

God and was filled with the Holy Spirit, but he had to act by faith.

The twenty-first century Church is seeking empowered servant leaders who will lead her to greater heights. The Church needs a new generation of leaders who have encountered God and have been empowered by the Holy Spirit. Only then will the Church be able to take the necessary steps of faith to overcome the obstacles on her journey to the City whose builder and maker is God.

CHAPTER 10

A CALL TO EXCELLENCE

I want to conclude this book by calling all Christian ministers to a more excellent level of ministry. I want to invite current theological students to seek this same degree of excellence in their future ministry, and to prepare for it to the best of their abilities. Unfortunately, I have witnessed less than excellent ministry in many parts of the world. While many faithful ministers of the Gospel hold a very high standard for themselves, there are also ministers who preach unprepared sermons, teach superficial lessons, neglect the healing ministry of Jesus, and provide weak leadership. I have observed substandard ministries in both small churches and megachurches alike. While small churches cite their lack of resources as an excuse for substandard ministry, megachurches attribute their weaknesses to the volume of members they serve. Nonetheless, the quality of ministry should be a matter of the minister's convictions, and the size of a church should not determine the quality of its ministry.

This book presents a multifaceted, biblical definition of Spirit-filled ministry, based on the ministry of Jesus and the apostles. We have reviewed the ministry recorded in the book of Acts and have examined the great challenges confronting the Church and Christian ministers in the twenty-first century. It is a difficult task to translate the vital ministry of the apostolic age to our postmodern period. This can only be accomplished with the help of the Holy Spirit and through His refreshing, renewing, and empowering presence.

We have also examined the major tasks of ministry, which are preaching, teaching, healing, and leading. God is looking for Spirit-filled preachers who have a word for their time and place. He is seeking people who can exegete the Word and the world. Spirit-led preachers are capable of connecting the Word with the world in such a way that the Word impacts the inhabitants of that world. Even postmodernists seek a word from the Lord. Blessed are those who will hear that Word from God and deliver it faithfully in the power of the Holy Spirit.

Good preaching must be complemented by outstanding teaching. The teaching ministry of the church determines the level of discipleship among its members. As Jesus preached the Kingdom of God and taught the principles of Kingdom lifestyle, we also must preach the good news and teach Kingdom values in order to develop modern disciples. Only sound biblical teaching will motivate today's cultural Christians to grow in their faith and knowledge of the Lord Jesus Christ. God is seeking committed teachers who will inform and impart for the purpose of spiritual transformation, but the Holy Spirit is the supreme instructor. Good teachers must depend on the Holy Spirit for wisdom, revelation, and discernment. These Spirit-led teachers enable their students to experience the renewal of their minds and the transformation of their lives.

Our broken world needs healers who move in the power of the Holy Spirit. Tired of self-help efforts and custom-made religions, people are seeking true healing for their shattered lives. Spirit-led ministers must offer them the healing power of Jesus, so that the body of Christ embodies a healing community. Pastors must involve church members in the healing ministry, so that all members of the body, not just ordained ministers, engage themselves in this healing work. Each member can be trained to minister healing in body, mind, spirit, and relationships. I call the Church of Jesus Christ to excellence in healing ministry.

America is experiencing a national shortage of ethical leaders. It has become clear that this shortage is particularly acute in business, politics, and government. The Church is also in need of strong leaders to guide her through the challenges of the new century. These tasks require men and women in leadership who have encountered God and have experienced the anointing of the Holy Spirit. The body of Christ does not need tyrants or dictators; it needs apostles, prophets, evangelists, pastors, teachers, and other ministers who are led by the Spirit. I call ministers to excellence in leadership.

As a minister of the Gospel and an individual who trains Spirit-led ministers, I present this concern for excellence in ministry with much optimism because history attests that God always finds the human vessels He requires to fulfill His purposes in the world. Extraordinary individuals, such as Saint Paul, Saint Augustine, Calvin, Luther, and Wesley, as well as ordinary persons such as Peter, James, Carey, and Seymour, were available to Him. God still wants to share the good news of Jesus Christ with the world. Those of us who are called to work with God on this project should consider ourselves very fortunate. May we give Him our very best, and may this be our prayer as we look into the future: Come, Holy Spirit! Come and lead us!

NOTES

Chapter 1

[1] H. Richard Niebuhr, *The Purpose of the Church and Its Ministry* (New York: Harper & Row, 1956), 64.
[2] David W. Bennett, *Metaphors of Ministry* (Grand Rapids: Baker, 1993), 53-54.
[3] David McKenna, *Renewing Our Ministry* (Waco: Word Books, 1986), 9.
[4] John W. Frye, *Jesus the Pastor* (Grand Rapids: Zondervan, 2000), 50-54.
[5] Henri Nouwen, *Creative Ministry* (Garden City, NY: Doubleday & Company, 1971).
[6] Victor Paul Furnish, "Theology and Ministry in the Pauline Letters," in *A Biblical Basis for Ministry*, ed. Earl E. Shelp and Ronald Sunderland (Philadelphia: Westminster Press, 1981), 128-136.
[7] H. Richard Niebuhr, 66-74.
[8] Samuel Southard, *Pastoral Authority in Personal Relationships* (Nashville: Abingdon, 1969), 20-21.
[9] Ibid., 14.

Chapter 2

[1] Charles A. Ver Straten, *A Caring Church* (Grand Rapids: Baker, 1988), 146.
[2] James F. Stitzinger, "Pastoral Ministry in History," in John A. MacArthur, Jr. (Ed.) *Rediscovering Pastoral Ministry* (Dallas: Word, 1995), 42.
[3] Thomas C. Oden, *Classical Pastoral Care,* 4 vols., (Grand Rapids: Baker, 1987).
[4] Oden, vol. 1, 13.
[5] Ibid., 13.
[6] Ibid., 42.
[7] Ibid., 43.
[8] Eddie Hyatt, *2000 Years of Charismatic Christianity* (Tulsa: Hyatt International Ministries, 1996).
[9] Oden, vol. 1, 149.
[10] Ibid., 160.
[11] Stitzinger, 52.
[12] Oden, vol. 2, 171.
[13] Oden, vol. 3, 28.
[14] Ibid., 200.
[15] Oden, vol. 4, 71.
[16] Stitzinger, 53.
[17] H. Richard Niebuhr and Daniel D. Williams, eds., *The Ministry in Historical Perspective* (San Francisco: Harper and Row, 1983), 199.
[18] Ibid., 194.
[19] Ibid., 196.
[20] William D. Salsbery, *Equipping and Mobilizing Believers to Perform a Shared Ministry of Pastoral Care,* D. Min. proj. (Tulsa: Oral Roberts University, 1991), 44.
[21] William A. Clebsch and Charles R. Jaekle, *Pastoral Care in Historical Perspective* (New York: Jason Aronson, 1975), 32-66.

[22] Niebuhr, 228.
[23] Sydney E. Mead, "The Rise of the Evangelical Conception of the Ministry in America: 1607-1850" in Niebuhr, 244.
[24] Robert S. Michaelsen, "Protestant Ministry in America: 1850-1950" in Niebuhr, 250.
[25] Joseph C. Hough, Jr. and John B. Cobb, Jr., *Christian Identity and Theological Education* (Chicago: Scholars Press, 1985), 5-6.
[26] H. Richard Niebuhr, *The Purpose of the Church and Its Ministry* (New York: Harper & Row, 1956), 51.

Chapter 3

[1] Donald E. Messer, *Contemporary Images of Christian Ministry* (Nashville: Abingdon, 1989).
[2] William Willimon, *Pastor: The Theology and Practice of Ordained Ministry* (Nashville, Abingdon, 2000).
[3] Leith Anderson, *Dying for Change* (Minneapolis: Bethany House, 1990).
[4] Ibid., 159.
[5] Ibid., 139-147.
[6] David Fisher, *21st Century Pastor* (Grand Rapids: Zondervan, 1996).
[7] John A. Sanford, *Ministry Burnout* (New York: Paulist, 1982), 5-16.
[8] Erla Zwingle, "A World Together," *National Geographic* (August 1999), 28.
[9] Erik Erikson, *Identity: Youth and Crisis* (New York: W.W. Norton & Company, 1968).

Chapter 4

[1] Henri Nouwen, *The Wounded Healer* (Garden City, NY: Doubleday, 1979).
[2] Abraham Maslow, *Motivation and Personality* (New York: Harper & Row, 1970), 35-47.
[3] Robert Coleman, *The Masterplan of Discipleship* (Grand Rapids: Baker, 1998).
[4] Charles V. Gerkin, *An Introduction to Pastoral Care* (Nashville: Abingdon, 1997).
[5] Peter Wagner, *Your Church Can Grow* (Glendale: Regal Books, 1976).
[6] Earl E. Shelp and Ronald H. Sunderland, eds., *Pastor as Priest* (New York: Pilgrim Press, 1987).

Chapter 5

[1] Paul Pruyser, *The Minister as Diagnostician* (Philadelphia: Westminster, 1976).
[2] Herbert Anderson, *The Family and Pastoral Care* (Philadelphia: Fortress, 1989), 35-39.
[3] Peter Martin, *A Marital Therapy Manual* (New York: Brunner/ Mazel, 1976), 15-33.
[4] Anderson, 83-106.
[5] Christie Cozad Neuger, "Pastoral Counseling With Women," *Clergy Journal* 71, no. 1 (1994): 5-8.
[6] Duane Parker, "Executive Director Notes," *Association of Clinical Pastoral Education News* (October, 1989): 3-4.
[7] Kay Marshall Storm, *Women in Crisis* (Michigan: Ministry Resource Library, 1986).
[8] Andrew Lester, *Pastoral Care With Children in Crisis* (Philadelphia: Westminster, 1985).

[9] Robert T. Frerichs, "A History of the Continuing Education Movement," *The Drew Gateway* 47, no. 1 (1976-77): 1-9.

[10] James Berkley, "The Unfinished Pastor," *Leadership* 5, no. 4 (1984): 128-129.

[11] Connolly C. Gamble, Jr., "Continuing Education for Ministry: Perspectives and Prospects," *The Drew Gateway* 47, no. 1 (1976-77): 10-19. And "Continuing Education: The Contemporary Scene," *The Drew Gateway* 47, no. 1 (1976-77): 37-47.

[12] Charles B. Fortier, "A Study of Continuing Education Needs of Clergymen in Lafayette Parish, Louisiana" (Doctoral Dissertation, Louisiana State University, 1972), *Dissertation Abstract International* 33, no.12A, 6589.

[13] Donald Emler, "Mid-career Development of United Methodist Parish Ministers within the State University System of Continuing Education," (Doctoral Dissertation, Indiana University, 1973), *Dissertation Abstract International* 3, no. 08, 4555.

[14] Jimmy W. Walker, "The Relationship of Continuing Professional Education and Pastoral Tenure among Southern Baptist Pastors," (Doctoral Dissertation, Texas State University, 1986), *Dissertation Abstract International* 47, no. 08A, 2855.

[15] Thomson K. Mathew, "Development and Validation of an Instrument to Measure the Continuing Education Needs of Professional Chaplains" (Ed.D. diss., Oklahoma State Univ., 1992).

Chapter 6

[1] John Stott, *Between Two Worlds* (Grand Rapids: W.B. Eerdmans, 1982), 181.

[2] William Hendriksen, *New Testament Commentary: The Gospel of Luke*, (Baker Book House, 1981), 351.
[3] William Willimon, *Pastor: The Theology and Practice of Ordained Ministry* (Nashville, Abingdon, 2000), 77.
[4] Aldwin Ragoonath, *How Shall They Hear?* (North Brunswick, NJ: Bridge-Logos, 1996), 4.
[5] Ralph G. Turnbull, *A History of Preaching*, vol. 3 (Grand Rapids: Baker, 1976), 163-171.
[6] Gerhard Friedrich, ed., *Theological Dictionary of the New Testament*, vol. 6 (Grand Rapids: W.B. Eerdmans, 1968), 781-862.
[7] Ragoonath, 63-88.
[8] Gijsbert D.J. Dingemans, "A Hearer in the Pew: Homiletical Reflections and Suggestions," in *Preaching as a Theological Task: A Collection of Essays in Honor of George Buttrick*, eds. Thomas G. Long and Ed Farley (Louisville: Westminster, 1996), 38-49.
[9] Bill Easum, "Ancient Mission in the Contemporary World," *Circuit Rider*, July/August 2002, 24-26.
[11] Rick Warren, "A Primer on Preaching Like Jesus," *REV*, March/ April 2002, 45-50.
[11] Tim Timmons, "Preaching to Convince," ed. James D. Berkley (Waco: Word, 1986), 20; quoted in Calvin Miller, *Market Place Preaching* (Grand Rapids: Baker, 1995), 18-19.
[12] Edwin C. Dargon, *A Brief History of Great Preaching*, vol. 1 (New York: Burt Franklin, 1968), 37.
[13] David Martyn Lloyd-Jones, *Studies in the Sermon on the Mount*, vol. 2 (Grand Rapids: W.B. Eerdmans, 1962), vii.
[14] Dennis F. Kinlaw, *Preaching in the Spirit* (Grand Rapids: Francis Asbury Press, 1985), 11.
[15] Juan Carlos Ortiz, *Disciple* (Carol Stream: Creation House, 1975), 60-64.

Chapter 7

[1] Lawrence Richards, *You, the Teacher* (Chicago: Moody Press, 1972), 66-67.
[2] Ronald G. Held, *Learning Together* (Springfield: Gospel Publishing House, 1976), 34.
[3] Leonard Sweet, *Postmodern Pilgrims: First Century Passion for the Twenty-first Century Church* (Nashville: Broadman & Holman, 2000).
[4] Malcolm S. Knowles, *Self-Directed Learning* (New York: Cambridge Book Company, 1988), 19.
[5] Ibid., 59-63.
[6] Benjamin Bloom, *Taxonomy of Educational Objectives* (New York: Longman, Green, and Co., 1956).
[7] Raymond Wlodkowski, *Enhancing Adult Motivation to Learn* (San Francisco: Jossey-Bass, 1988).
[8] Richard Paul and Linda Elder, *A Miniature Guide for Those Who Teach on How to Improve Student Learning* (Dillon Beach, CA: Foundation for Critical Thinking, 2002).
[9] Carnegie S. Calian, *The Ideal Seminary* (Louisville: Westminster John Knox Press, 2001), 37.

Chapter 8

[1] William A. Clebsch and Charles R. Jaekle, *Pastoral Care in Historical Perspective* (New York: Jason Aronson, 1975).
[2] Thomas C. Oden, *Classical Pastoral Care*, 4 vols. (Grand Rapids: Baker, 1987).
[3] Thomson K. Mathew, *Ministry Between Miracles* (Fairfax: Xulon, 2002).
[4] William Hulme, *Pastoral Care and Counseling* (Minneapolis: Augsburg, 1981).

Chapter 9

[1] Bruce Goettsche, *Principles of Effective Christian Leadership* [online]; available from http://www.unionchurch.com/archive/050398.html.
[2] Warren G. Bennis and Burt Nanus, *Leaders: The Strategy for Taking Charge* (New York: Harper, 1997).
[3] Robert Webber, *The Younger Evangelicals: Facing the Challenges of the New World* (Grand Rapids: Baker, 2002).
[4] Edward Bratcher, *Walk on Water Syndrome* (Grand Rapids: Word, 1984).
[5] Gordon Fee, *Gospel and Spirit* (Peabody: Hendrickson, 1991), 120-143.
[6] Oral Roberts, *Expect A Miracle* (Nashville: Thomas Nelson, 1995).
[7] Edward Bratcher, *Walk on Water Syndrome* (Grand Rapids: Word, 1984).
[8] John Kotter, *Leading Change* (Boston: Harvard Business School Press, 1996).
[9] Kenneth O. Gangel, *Feeding and Leading* (Wheaton: Scripture Press, 1989), 189.
[10] John Lawyer and Neil Katz, *Communication Skills for Ministry* (Dubuque: Kendall/ Hunt, 1983), 37-38.
[11] J. Robert Clinton, *The Making of a Leader* (Colorado Springs: NavPress, 1988).
[12] Henri Nouwen, *The Wounded Healer* (Garden City: Image Books, 1979).

BIBLIOGRAPHY

Anderson, Herbert. *The Family and Pastoral Care.* Philadelphia: Fortress, 1989.

Anderson, Leith. *Dying for Change.* Minneapolis: Bethany House, 1990.

Bennis, Warren G., and Burt Nanus. *Leaders: The Strategy for Taking Charge.* New York: Harper, 1997. *Dissertation Abstract International* 33, no.12A, 6589.

Berkley, James. "The Unfinished Pastor," *Leadership* 5, no. 4 (1984): 128-129.

Bloom, Benjamin S. *Taxonomy of Educational Objectives.* New York: Longman, Green, and Co., 1956.

Bratcher, Edward. *Walk on Water Syndrome.* Grand Rapids: Word, 1984.

Calian, Carnegie S. *The Ideal Seminary.* Louisville: Westminster John Knox Press, 2001.

Clebsch, William A., and Charles R. Jaekle. *Pastoral Care in Historical Perspective.* New York: Jason Aronson, 1975.

Clinton, J. Robert. *The Making of a Leader.* Colorado Springs: NavPress, 1988.

Coleman, Robert. *The Masterplan of Discipleship.* Grand Rapids: Baker, 1998.

Dargon, Edwin C. *A Brief History of Great Preaching.* Vol. 1. New York: Burt Franklin, 1968.

Dingemans, Gijsbert D. J. "A Hearer in the Pew: Homiletical Reflections and Suggestions." In *Preaching as a Theological Task: A Collection of Essays in Honor of George Buttrick,* ed. Thomas G. Long and Ed Farley, 38-49. Louisville: Westminster, 1996.

Easum, Bill. "Ancient Mission in the Contemporary World." *Circuit Rider,* July/August 2002, 24-26.

Emler, Donald. "Mid-Career Development of United Methodist Parish Ministers Within the State University System of Continuing Education." Ph.D. diss., Indiana University, 1973. In *Dissertation Abstract International* 3, no. 8, 4555.

Erikson, Erik. *Identity: Youth and Crisis.* New York: W.W. Norton & Company, 1968.

Fee, Gordon. *Gospel and Spirit.* Peabody: Hendrickson, 1991.

Fisher, David. *The Twenty-First Century Pastor*. Grand Rapids: Zondervan, 1996.

Fortier, Charles B. "A Study of Continuing Education Needs of Clergymen in Lafayette Parish, Louisiana." Ph.D. diss., Louisiana State University, 1972. In *Dissertation Abstract International* 33, no 12A, 6589.

Frerichs, Robert T. "A History of the Continuing Education Movement." *The Drew Gateway* 47, no. 1 (1976-77): 1-9.

Friedrich, Gerhard, ed. *Theological Dictionary of the New Testament*, Vol. 6. Grand Rapids: W.B. Eerdmans, 1968.

Gamble, Connolly C., Jr. "Continuing Education for Ministry: Perspectives and Prospects." *The Drew Gateway* 47, no. 1 (1976-77): 10-19.

_____. "Continuing Education: The Contemporary Scene." *The Drew Gateway* 47, no. 1 (1976-77): 37-47.

Gangel, Kenneth O. *Feeding and Leading*. Wheaton: Scripture Press, 1989.

Gerkin, Charles V. *An Introduction to Pastoral Care*. Nashville: Abingdon, 1997.

Goettsche, Bruce. *Principles of Effective Christian Leadership*. [online]; available from http://www.unionchurch.com/archive/050398.html

Held, Ronald G. *Learning Together*. Springfield: Gospel, 1976.

Hendrickson, William. *New Testament Commentary*: *The Gospel of Luke,* Grand Rapids:
Baker Book House, 1981, 351.

Hulme, William. *Pastoral Care and Counseling*. Minneapolis: Augsburg, 1981.

Hyatt, Eddie. *2000 Years of Charismatic Christianity*. Tulsa, OK: Hyatt International Ministries, 1996.

Kinlaw, Dennis F. *Preaching in the Spirit*. Grand Rapids: Francis Asbury Press, 1985.

Knowles, Malcolm S. *Self-Directed Learning*. Englewood Cliffs, NJ: Prentice Hall Regents, 1975.

Kotter, John. *Leading Change*. Boston: Harvard Business School Press, 1996.

Lawyer, John, and Neil Katz. *Communication Skills for Ministry*. Dubuque: Kendall/Hunt, 1983.

Lester, Andrew. *Pastoral Care With Children in Crisis*. Philadelphia: Westminster, 1985.

Lloyd-Jones, David Martyn. *Studies in the Sermon on the Mount*, Vol. 2. Grand Rapids: W.B. Eerdmans, 1962.

MacArthur, John A., Jr. *Rediscovering Pastoral Ministry*. Dallas: Word, 1995.

Martin, Peter. *A Marital Therapy Manual.* New York: Brunner/Mazel, 1976.

Maslow, Abraham. *Motivation and Personality.* New York: Harper & Row, 1970.

Mathew, Thomson K. *Ministry Between Miracles.* Fairfax: Xulon, 2002.

Mathew, Thomson K. "Development and Validation of an Instrument to Measure the Continuing Education Needs of Professional Chaplains." Ed.D. diss., Oklahoma State University, 1992.

Mead, Sydney E. "The Rise of the Evangelical Conception of the Ministry in America: 1607-1850." In *The Ministry in Historical Perspective*, ed. H. Richard Niebuhr and Daniel D. Williams, 207-249. San Francisco: Harper and Row, 1983.

Messer, Donald E. *Contemporary Images of Christian Minister.* Nashville: Abingdon, 1989.

Michaelsen, Robert S. "Protestant Ministry in America: 1850-1950," In *The Ministry in Historical Perspective*, ed. H. Richard Niebuhr and Daniel D. Williams, 250-288. San Francisco: Harper and Row, 1983.

Neuger, Christie Cozad. "Pastoral Counseling with Women." *Clergy Journal* 71, no. 1 (1994): 5-8.

Niebuhr, H. Richard, and Daniel D. Williams, eds. *The Ministry in Historical Perspective.* San Francisco: Harper and Row, 1983.

Nouwen, Henri. *The Wounded Healer*. Garden City: Image Books, Doubleday, 1979.

Oden, Thomas C. *Classical Pastoral Care*. Vol. 1. Grand Rapids: Baker, 1987.
_____. *Classical Pastoral Care*. Vol. 2. Grand Rapids: Baker, 1987.
_____. *Classical Pastoral Care*. Vol. 3. Grand Rapids: Baker, 1987.
_____. *Classical Pastoral Care*. Vol. 4. Grand Rapids: Baker, 1987.

Ortiz, Juan Carlos. *Disciple*. Carol Stream, IL: Creation House, 1975.

Parker, Duane. "Executive Director Notes." *Association of Clinical Pastoral Education News* (October 1989): 3-4.

Paul, Richard, and Linda Elder. *A Miniature Guide for Those Who Teach on How to Improve Student Learning*. United States of America: Foundation for Critical Thinking.

Pruyser, Paul. *The Minister as Diagnostician*. Philadelphia: Westminster, 1976.

Ragoonath, Aldwin. *How Shall They Hear?* North Brunswick, NJ: Bridge-Logos, 1996.

Richards, Lawrence. *You, the Teacher*. Chicago: Moody Press, 1972.

Roberts, Oral. *Expect A Miracle*. Nashville: Thomas Nelson, 1995.

Salsbery, William D. "Equipping and Mobilizing Believers to Perform a Shared Ministry of Pastoral Care." D. Min. diss., Oral Roberts University, 1991.

Sanford, John A. *Ministry Burnout*. New York: Paulist, 1982.

Shelp, Earl E., and Ronald H. Sunderland, eds. *Pastor as Priest*. New York: Pilgrim Press, 1987.

Stitzinger, James F. "Pastoral Ministry in History." In *Rediscovering Pastoral Ministry*, ed. John A. MacArthur, Jr. Dallas: Word, 1995.

Storm, Kay Marshall. *Women in Crisis*. Michigan: Ministry Resource Library, 1986.

Stott, John. *Between Two Worlds*. Grand Rapids: W.B. Eerdmans, 1982.

Sweet, Leonard. *Postmodern Pilgrims: First Century Passion for the Twenty-First Century Church*. Nashville: Broadman & Holman, 2000.

Timmons, Tim. "Preaching to Convince." ed. James D. Berkley. Waco: Word, 1986. Quoted in Calvin Miller, *Market Place Preaching*, 18-19, Grand Rapids: Baker, 1995.

Turnbull, Ralph G. *A History of Preaching,* Vol. 3. Grand Rapids: Baker, 1976.

Ver Straten, Charles A. *A Caring Church*. Grand Rapids: Baker, 1988.

Walker, Jimmy W. "The Relationship of Continuing Professional Education and Pastoral Tenure Among Southern Baptist Pastors." Ph. D. diss., Texas State University, 1986. In *Dissertation Abstract International* 47, no. 08A, 2855.

Webber, Robert. *The Younger Evangelicals: Facing the Challenges of the New World*. Grand Rapids: Baker, 2002.

Wagner, Peter. *Your Church Can Grow*. Glendale: Regal Books, G/L Publications, 1976.

Warren, Rick."A Primer on Preaching Like Jesus." *REV* March/April 2002, 45-50.

Willimon, William. *Pastor: The Theology and Practice of Ordained Ministry*. Nashville: Abingdon, 2000.

Wlodkowski, Raymond. *Enhancing Adult Motivation to Learn*. San Francisco: Jossey-Bass, 1988.

Zwingle, Erla. "A World Together." *National Geographic* 196, August 1999, 12-33.

Another book, *Ministry Between Miracles*, by Thomson K. Mathew is available from Xulon Press. You may order by calling 1-866-909-BOOK (2665).

You may respond to the author by writing to:

>Dr. Thomson K. Mathew
>School of Theology and Missions
>Oral Roberts University
>7777 South Lewis Avenue
>Tulsa, OK 74171, U.S.A.
>
>Email: stm@oru.edu
>Telephone: (918) 495-6161